Dolomites Trav

"Explore Dolomites, Your Essential Guide to the Captivating Alpine Lakes"

Lawrence B. Gibson

All rights reserved. No part of this publication may be reproduced, distributed, or transmitted in any form or by any means, including photocopying, recording, or other electronic or mechanical methods, without the prior written permission of the publisher, except in the case of brief quotations embodied in critical reviews and certain other noncommercial uses permitted by copyright law.

Copyright © *Lawrence B. Gibson, 2024*

Table of Contents

Introduction

Welcome to the Dolomites
Overview of the Dolomite Region
Best Time to Visit
How to Get There
Accommodation Options
Essential Packing List
Safety Tips and Guidelines
Local Cuisine and Restaurants

The Dolomites at a Glance

History and Geology
Culture and Traditions
Flora and Fauna

The Walks

Walk 1 Lago di Braies
Walk 2 Rifugio Biella Loop
Walk 3 Monte Specie
Walk 4 Alpe di Sennes Circuit
Walk 5 Landro to Cortina on the Old Railway Line
Walk 6 Torre dei Scarperi Circuit
Walk 7 The Val Fiscalina Tour
Walk 8 The Tre Cime di Lavaredo Loop
Walk 9 Through the Cadini di Misurina
Walk 10 Monte Piana
Walk 11 Lago di Misurina
Walk 12 Val Popena Alta
Walk 13 Rifugio Vandelli Traverse
Walk 14 Forcella Zumèles and the Cristallo
Walk 15 Below the Antelao
Walk 16 Rifugio Padova and Rifugio Tita Barba
Walk 17 The Pramper Circuit
Walk 18 Lago Coldai and the Civetta
Walk 19 The Pelmo Tour
Walk 20 Gores de Federa
Walk 21 Around the Croda da Lago
Walk 22 The Cinque Torri
Walk 23 Up the Nuvolau
Walk 24 Skirting the Tofana di Rozes
Walk 25 The Lagazuoi Tunnels
Walk 26 The Kaiserjäger Route

Walk 27 Round the Settsass
Walk 28 Santa Croce Sanctuary.
Walk 29 Sass de Putia
Walk 30 Sentiero delle Odle
Walk 31 The Rasciesa Ridge
Walk 32 Across the Puez-Odle Altopiano
Walk 33 The Bullaccia Tour
Walk 34 Alpe di Siusi Circuit and Rifugio BolzanoWalk 35 Castel Presule
Walk 36 Val Ciamin
Walk 37 The Inner Catinaccio
Walk 38 Sentiero del Masaré
Walk 39 The Latemar Labyrinth and Lago di Carezza
Walk 40 Circumnavigating Sassopiatto-Sassolungo
Walk 41 The Sella and Piz Boë
Walk 42 Viel del Pan
Walk 43 The Sas de Adam Crest
Walk 44 The Marmolada and Punta Serauta
Walk 45 Rifugio Falier in Valle Ombretta

Practical Information

Transportation Tips
Local Etiquette and Customs
Emergency Contacts and Services
Useful Phrases in Italian and German
Travel Insurance

Maps and Resources

Regional Maps
Trail Maps
Recommended Apps and Websites.

Introduction

Welcome to the Dolomites! I'm Lawrence B. Gibson, your guide through one of the most breathtaking regions in the world. Nestled in northern Italy, the Dolomites are a paradise for nature lovers, hikers, and anyone looking to immerse themselves in stunning landscapes and rich culture.

The Dolomites are a UNESCO World Heritage site, celebrated for their unique geological formations, striking pinnacles, and vibrant alpine meadows. The area is a playground for outdoor enthusiasts, offering endless opportunities for walking, climbing, and skiing. Each season transforms the Dolomites, from the lush greens of summer to the snow-covered peaks of winter, providing a different, yet equally enchanting, experience.

This guide is designed to help you make the most of your visit. Whether you are an experienced hiker or a casual walker, this guide offers a carefully curated selection of walks, from leisurely lakeside strolls to challenging mountain circuits. Each walk is detailed with route descriptions, highlights, and practical tips to ensure you are well-prepared and can enjoy the stunning scenery safely.

Benefits of Using This Guide:

Comprehensive Walks: With 50 meticulously planned walks, this guide caters to all levels of fitness and experience. Each walk includes detailed directions, estimated times, and points of interest, making it easy to choose an adventure that suits your preferences.

Insider Tips: Having explored the Dolomites extensively, I share insider knowledge on the best viewpoints, hidden gems, and local secrets that you won't find in typical tourist guides. These tips will enhance your experience and help you discover the true essence of the Dolomites.

Practical Information: From packing lists to safety guidelines, this guide is packed with practical advice to help you prepare for your trip. You'll find essential information on local customs, transportation options, and useful phrases in Italian and German to help you navigate the region with ease.

Cultural Insights: Beyond the natural beauty, the Dolomites are rich in culture and history. This guide delves into the region's fascinating past, vibrant traditions, and delectable cuisine, providing a deeper understanding and appreciation of the area.

How to Use This Guide:

Start by reading through the introductory sections to get a sense of what the Dolomites have to offer and how to prepare for your journey. Then, explore the detailed walk descriptions to plan your daily adventures. Each walk is accompanied by a map and practical advice to help you navigate the trails confidently.

Use the practical information sections to familiarize yourself with local etiquette, emergency contacts, and transportation tips. The maps and resources section offers additional tools to aid your planning and ensure you have everything you need at your fingertips.

The Dolomites are a place that captivates and inspires. With their dramatic landscapes, charming villages, and warm hospitality, they offer an experience unlike any other. This guide is your companion, crafted to help you explore, appreciate, and fall in love with the Dolomites.

Join me, Lawrence B. Gibson, on this journey through one of the most beautiful places on Earth. Let's discover the magic of the Dolomites together.

Overview of the Dolomite Region.

The Dolomites, also known as the "Pale Mountains," are a mountain range located in northeastern Italy. They form part of the Southern Limestone Alps and are spread across the provinces of Belluno, South Tyrol, and Trentino. Renowned for their dramatic landscapes, the Dolomites offer a unique blend of natural beauty, cultural richness, and outdoor adventure opportunities.

Geography and Landscape

The Dolomites cover an area of approximately 142,000 hectares and are characterized by their distinctive geological formations. The mountains are composed mainly of dolomite rock, which gives them their characteristic pale color and rugged appearance. The region boasts a variety of landscapes, including towering peaks, deep valleys, lush meadows, and serene alpine lakes.

Key geographic features of the Dolomites include:

> Tre Cime di Lavaredo: Iconic three-peaked mountain that is a symbol of the Dolomites.
> Marmolada: The highest peak in the Dolomites, standing at 3,343 meters (10,968 feet).
> Sella Group: A massif known for its imposing cliffs and high-altitude plateau.
> Civetta and Pelmo: Two striking mountains often referred to as the "Twin Towers" of the Dolomites.

Climate

The Dolomites experience a varied climate due to their elevation and geographical location. Summers are generally mild, with temperatures ranging from 15°C to 25°C (59°F to 77°F) in the valleys, making it an ideal time for hiking and outdoor activities. Winters are cold, with temperatures often dropping below freezing, creating perfect conditions for skiing and snowboarding.

The region receives significant snowfall in winter, and the higher elevations can remain snow-covered well into the spring. Rainfall is more frequent in the summer months, but the weather can change rapidly, so visitors should always be prepared for varying conditions.

Flora and Fauna

The diverse climate and terrain of the Dolomites support a rich variety of plant and animal life. The lower altitudes are covered with dense forests of pine, fir, and larch, while the higher altitudes feature alpine meadows adorned with colorful wildflowers. Some notable flora includes the edelweiss, gentian, and the Dolomite bellflower.

The region is also home to a wide range of wildlife. Visitors might spot animals such as:

Chamois: A type of mountain goat-antelope found in rocky areas.

Marmots: Large, burrowing rodents often seen in alpine meadows.

Golden Eagles: Majestic birds of prey that soar above the mountain peaks.

Red Deer and Roe Deer: Common in the forests and lower slopes.

Best Time to Visit

The Dolomites offer something for everyone throughout the year, but choosing the best time to visit depends on your interests and the type of experience you're seeking. Whether you're planning a family vacation, an adventure-packed trip, a sightseeing tour, or a peaceful retreat away from the crowds, this guide will help you determine the ideal time for your visit.

Family Vacations

Summer (June to August): Summer is the best time for a family vacation in the Dolomites. The weather is mild, with temperatures ranging from 15°C to 25°C (59°F to 77°F), making it perfect for outdoor activities like hiking, cycling, and picnicking. Many trails are accessible for families, including those with young children, and there are numerous family-friendly attractions such as adventure parks, swimming in alpine lakes, and exploring charming villages.

Spring (April to May) and Autumn (September to October): These shoulder seasons are also excellent for family trips. The weather is cooler, but the scenery is stunning with blooming flowers in spring and vibrant foliage in autumn. These periods offer a quieter experience with fewer tourists, allowing families to enjoy the natural beauty and local attractions more peacefully.

Adventure Seekers

Summer (June to September): This is the peak season for adventure seekers. The long daylight hours and favorable weather conditions provide ample opportunities for hiking, rock climbing, via ferrata, mountain biking, and paragliding. The Dolomites' extensive network of trails and climbing routes cater to all skill levels, from beginners to seasoned adventurers.

Winter (December to March): Winter transforms the Dolomites into a playground for snow sports enthusiasts. Skiing, snowboarding, snowshoeing, and ice climbing are popular activities. The region is home to some of the best ski resorts in the world, with well-groomed slopes, modern facilities, and breathtaking views. Adventure seekers can also enjoy cross-country skiing and backcountry tours for a more off-the-beaten-path experience.

Sightseeing Tourists

Spring (April to June) and Autumn (September to November): These periods are ideal for sightseeing tourists. The weather is generally pleasant, and the crowds are smaller compared to the peak summer season. Spring offers lush green landscapes and blooming flowers, while autumn provides a spectacular display of fall colors. These seasons are perfect for exploring the Dolomites' picturesque villages, historical sites, and cultural events.

Winter (December to March): Winter is also a magical time for sightseeing, with the landscape covered in snow, creating a picturesque winter wonderland. The Christmas markets, festive decorations, and winter events add a special charm to the region. This is a great time to visit for those who enjoy the cozy atmosphere and winter scenery.

Less Crowded Times

Spring (April to May) and Autumn (October to November): These shoulder seasons are the best times to visit if you want to avoid the crowds. The trails, attractions, and accommodations are less crowded, allowing for a more relaxed and intimate experience. The weather can be variable, so it's important to be prepared for cooler temperatures and occasional rain, but the tranquility and beauty of the Dolomites during these times are well worth it.

Early Summer (June) and Late Summer (September): Visiting at the beginning or end of the summer season offers a balance between favorable weather and fewer tourists. June offers beautiful wildflowers and lush greenery, while September provides warm days and cool nights, with the added bonus of the autumnal foliage starting to appear.

Summary

Best Time for Families: Summer (June to August), Spring (April to May), and Autumn (September to October).

Best Time for Adventure Seekers: Summer (June to September) and Winter (December to March).

Best Time for Sightseeing Tourists: Spring (April to June), Autumn (September to November), and Winter (December to March).

Best Time to Avoid Crowds: Spring (April to May), Autumn (October to November), Early Summer (June), and Late Summer (September).

The Dolomites are a year-round destination, offering unique and memorable experiences in every season. Whether you're looking for family fun, thrilling adventures, cultural exploration, or peaceful solitude, the Dolomites have the perfect time and setting for your visit. Plan your trip according to your interests and preferences, and you're sure to have an unforgettable experience in this stunning region.

Activity Calendar For The Dolomites.

Month	Unique Activity	How to Explore	Best Time to Visit
January	Skiing and Snowboarding	Visit top ski resorts like Cortina d'Ampezzo, Val Gardena, and Alta Badia. Enjoy well-groomed slopes and modern facilities.	Winter (December to March)
February	Snowshoeing and Winter Hiking	Explore snow-covered trails and pristine	Winter (December to March)

		landscapes on snowshoes. Guided tours available.	
March	Cross-Country Skiing	Discover extensive cross-country trails in Val di Fiemme and Alpe di Siusi. Ideal for all skill levels.	Winter (December to March)
April	Spring Wildflower Viewing	Hike in the lower valleys to see blooming wildflowers. Explore areas	Spring (April to May)

23

		like Val Gardena and Alpe di Siusi.	
May	Cycling and Mountain Biking	Ride through scenic routes like the Sella Ronda and Val Pusteria. Rent bikes locally.	Spring (April to June)
June	Hiking and Via Ferrata	Take advantage of long daylight hours to hike iconic trails like Tre Cime di Lavaredo and via ferrata routes.	Early Summer (June)

24

July	Paragliding and Adventure Sports	Experience paragliding in areas like Kronplatz. Try rock climbing, canyoning, and zip-lining.	Summer (June to August)
August	Exploring Alpine Lakes	Visit stunning lakes like Lago di Braies and Lago di Misurina. Perfect for swimming, boating, and picnicking.	Summer (June to August)

September	Autumn Foliage Hiking	Hike through forests with vibrant fall colors in areas like Val di Funes and Puez-Odle Altopiano.	Autumn (September to November)
October	Wine Tasting and Harvest Festivals	Visit vineyards and participate in harvest festivals. Explore wine regions like Trentino and Alto Adige.	Autumn (September to November)

26

		Relax in spa resorts offering thermal	
November	Spa and Wellness Retreats	baths, massages, and wellness treatments. Areas like Merano are ideal.	Autumn (October to November)
December	Christmas Markets and Festivities	Experience festive markets in towns like Bolzano, Bressanone, and Brunico. Enjoy local crafts, food,	Winter (December)

| | | and traditions. | |

How to Get There: Transportation Guide for the Dolomites.

The Dolomites are well-connected and accessible from several major cities and airports in Italy and neighboring countries. Here's a detailed transportation guide to help you plan your journey to the Dolomites, including the best flights and local transportation options.

Best Airports for Accessing the Dolomites
1. Venice Marco Polo Airport (VCE):

Location: Venice, Italy
Distance to Dolomites: Approximately 150-200 km (93-124 miles)
Best For: Southern and central Dolomites
Connections: Regular international and domestic flights. Major airlines and budget carriers operate here.

2. Verona Villafranca Airport (VRN):

Location: Verona, Italy
Distance to Dolomites: Approximately 150-200 km (93-124 miles)
Best For: Western Dolomites
Connections: Well-connected with European cities. Offers flights by major and low-cost airlines.

3. Innsbruck Airport (INN):

Location: Innsbruck, Austria

Distance to Dolomites: Approximately 100-150 km (62-93 miles)
Best For: Northern Dolomites
Connections: Regional and international flights, particularly from European destinations.

4. Milan Bergamo Airport (BGY):

Location: Bergamo, Italy
Distance to Dolomites: Approximately 200-300 km (124-186 miles)
Best For: Western Dolomites
Connections: Wide range of budget and regular flights from Europe.

5. Treviso Airport (TSF):

Location: Treviso, Italy

Distance to Dolomites: Approximately 150 km (93 miles)
Best For: Central Dolomites
Connections: Mainly budget airlines with European routes.

Getting to the Dolomites from the Airport

Car Rental:

Availability: All major airports have car rental services.
Best For: Flexibility and convenience in exploring the Dolomites.
Tips: Book in advance for the best rates. Ensure your rental includes insurance and understand the driving regulations in Italy.

Public Transportation:

Train: Italy has an extensive and efficient train network. From major airports, you can take a

train to key transit hubs like Bolzano, Trento, or Belluno, then transfer to regional trains or buses.
Venice to Bolzano/Trento: Frequent trains via Trenitalia or Italo.
Verona to Bolzano: Direct trains available.
Bus: From train stations, regional buses operated by companies like SAD, Dolomitibus, and FlixBus can take you to various towns in the Dolomites.
Shuttle Services: Some airports and major cities offer shuttle services directly to popular destinations in the Dolomites. Check local providers for schedules and bookings.

Private Transfers:

Availability: Private transfer services can be pre-booked for direct travel from the airport to your accommodation.
Best For: Convenience and comfort, especially for families or groups.

Local Transportation in the Dolomites

Buses:

Operators: SAD, Dolomitibus, and other local companies.
Coverage: Extensive network covering most towns and tourist spots.
Tips: Check schedules in advance, as some routes may have limited service, especially off-season.

Trains:

Operators: Trenitalia for regional routes.
Coverage: Main train lines connect major towns like Bolzano, Bressanone, and Brunico. Transfers to buses or local trains may be needed for smaller destinations.

Taxis and Ride-Sharing:

Availability: Taxis are available in towns and at train stations.

Ride-Sharing: Services like Uber may be limited, but local ride-sharing apps can be an option.

Cycling:

Rentals: Available in most towns. Biking is a popular way to explore the Dolomites, with many dedicated cycling paths.

Tips: Ensure you have proper gear and check the difficulty level of cycling routes.

Hiking:

Trails: Well-marked hiking trails connect many areas. Maps and guides are available locally.

Tips: Wear appropriate footwear and carry essentials like water, snacks, and weather-appropriate clothing.

Practical Tips

    Plan Ahead: Check transportation schedules and book tickets in advance, especially during peak seasons.

    Pack Smart: Bring appropriate clothing and gear for your planned activities.

    Stay Informed: Keep updated on local travel advisories and weather conditions.

    Language: While many locals speak English, learning basic Italian or German phrases can be helpful.

Accommodation Options in the Dolomites.

Here are ten unique accommodation options in the Dolomites, complete with updated information, addresses, and highlights.

1. **Hotel Cristallo, a Luxury Collection Resort & Spa**

   Location: Cortina d'Ampezzo
   Address: Via Rinaldo Menardi, 42, 32043 Cortina d'Ampezzo BL, Italy

Uniqueness: A five-star resort offering stunning views of the Dolomites, luxurious spa facilities, gourmet dining, and a rich history dating back to 1901.

2. **Rosa Alpina Hotel & Spa**

Location: San Cassiano
Address: Strada Micurà de Rü, 20, 39036 San Cassiano in Badia BZ, Italy
Uniqueness: Known for its blend of traditional Alpine charm and modern luxury, this hotel offers Michelin-starred dining, an award-winning spa, and proximity to ski slopes and hiking trails.

3. **Hotel La Perla**

Location: Corvara in Badia
Address: Col Alt, 105, 39033 Corvara in Badia BZ, Italy
Uniqueness: A family-run hotel with a focus on sustainability and local culture, featuring cozy, elegant rooms, a renowned restaurant, and access to the Sella Ronda ski circuit.

4. Alpina Dolomites Gardena Health Lodge & Spa

Location: Alpe di Siusi
Address: Compatsch, 39040 Alpe di Siusi BZ, Italy
Uniqueness: An eco-friendly lodge offering panoramic views of the Alpe di Siusi, comprehensive wellness programs, and direct access to hiking and skiing.

5. Hotel Ciasa Salares

Location: San Cassiano
Address: Strada Pre de Vi, 31, 39036 San Cassiano in Badia BZ, Italy
Uniqueness: A luxurious retreat featuring gourmet dining, including a famous cheese room, a relaxing spa, and beautifully appointed rooms reflecting local traditions.

6. ADLER Spa Resort Dolomiti

Location: Ortisei
Address: Via Rezia, 7, 39046 Ortisei BZ, Italy

Uniqueness: A wellness-focused resort with extensive spa facilities, thermal pools, and a holistic approach to health and relaxation, situated in the heart of the Val Gardena.

7. Hotel Sassongher

Location: Corvara in Badia
Address: Strada Sassongher, 45, 39033 Corvara in Badia BZ, Italy
Uniqueness: A luxurious and traditional hotel offering spacious rooms, a wellness center, and easy access to the Sella Ronda ski area.

8. Dolomiti Wellness Hotel Fanes

Location: San Cassiano
Address: Strada Pecei, 19, 39036 San Cassiano in Badia BZ, Italy
Uniqueness: Known for its wellness facilities, including a sky pool with panoramic mountain views, fine dining, and activities like guided hikes and skiing.

9. Forestis Dolomites

Location: **Brixen**
Address: **Palmschoß, 39042 Brixen BZ, Italy**
Uniqueness: A modern, luxury retreat nestled in the forest with a focus on wellness, featuring a sleek design, organic cuisine, and a tranquil setting perfect for relaxation.

10. **Parkhotel Holzner**

Location: **Soprabolzano**
Address: **Dorf, 18, 39054 Soprabolzano BZ, Italy**
Uniqueness: A historic hotel blending Art Nouveau charm with modern amenities, offering stunning views, gourmet dining, and activities for both families and couples.

These accommodations offer a mix of luxury, tradition, and unique experiences, ensuring a memorable stay in the Dolomites. Each location provides easy access to the region's natural beauty and outdoor activities, making them ideal bases for exploring this stunning area.

Essential Packing List for the Dolomites.

When preparing for a trip to the Dolomites, it's crucial to pack appropriately for the region's varying weather conditions and the activities you plan to undertake. Here's a comprehensive packing list to help ensure you have everything you need for a comfortable and enjoyable visit.

Clothing

Layered Clothing:
- Base Layers: Moisture-wicking tops and bottoms to keep you dry.
- Mid Layers: Insulating layers such as fleece or down jackets for warmth.
- Outer Layers: Waterproof and windproof jackets and pants to protect against rain and wind.

Footwear:
- Hiking Boots: Sturdy, waterproof boots with good ankle support for hiking.
- Casual Shoes: Comfortable shoes for walking around towns and villages.
- Sandals: For relaxing at your accommodation or for use in spa areas.

Accessories:
- Hats: A sun hat for summer and a warm hat for colder months.
- Gloves: Lightweight gloves for hiking and warmer gloves for winter.
- Scarves and Buffs: To protect against wind and cold.

Specialized Clothing:
- Swimwear: For swimming in alpine lakes or using spa facilities.
- Ski Gear: If visiting in winter, pack your ski jacket, pants, and other necessary ski equipment.

Gear and Equipment

Backpack: A comfortable daypack for carrying essentials on hikes.
Water Bottle: Reusable bottle to stay hydrated during activities.
Hiking Poles: Useful for stability and reducing strain on joints.
Maps and GPS: Physical maps and a GPS device or smartphone with offline maps.
Sunglasses: UV-protective sunglasses for sun protection.
Headlamp or Flashlight: For early morning or late evening hikes.
First Aid Kit: Basic first aid supplies, including bandages, antiseptic wipes, and any personal medications.
Multi-tool or Knife: Handy for various uses during hikes or camping.
Camera: To capture the stunning scenery and memorable moments.
Binoculars: For wildlife spotting and enjoying distant views.

Personal Items

Toiletries:

Toothbrush and toothpaste
Shampoo and conditioner
Soap or body wash
Deodorant
Hairbrush or comb

Sunscreen and Lip Balm: High SPF to protect against strong mountain sun.

Insect Repellent: Especially useful during the summer months.

Medications: Any personal medications, plus extras like pain relievers and motion sickness pills.

Documents and Money

Identification: Passport or ID card.

Travel Insurance: Printed copy of your travel insurance policy.

Credit Cards and Cash: Both are useful, as some remote areas may not accept cards.

Important Documents: Copies of reservations, maps, and emergency contacts.

Electronics

Smartphone and Charger: For navigation, communication, and taking photos.

Portable Power Bank: To keep your devices charged while on the go.

Adapters and Converters: For charging devices, especially if coming from outside Europe.

Laptop or Tablet: If you need to work or stay connected during your trip.

Seasonal Considerations

Winter: Additional thermal layers, ski equipment, and heavier gloves and hats.

Summer: Extra sun protection, lightweight clothing, and swimwear.

By packing these essentials, you'll be well-prepared for a safe and enjoyable adventure in the Dolomites, ready to explore everything this beautiful region has to offer.

Top Restaurants in the Dolomites.

Here's a list of top restaurants in the Dolomites, highlighting their unique features, addresses, and culinary offerings.

1. St. Hubertus

Location: San Cassiano
Address: Strada Micurà de Rü, 20, 39036 San Cassiano in Badia BZ, Italy
Uniqueness: This three-Michelin-starred restaurant, located in the Rosa Alpina Hotel, offers a refined culinary experience with a focus on local and sustainable ingredients. Chef Norbert Niederkofler's "Cook the Mountain"

philosophy emphasizes Alpine flavors and traditions.

2. **La Stüa de Michil**

Location: Corvara in Badia
Address: Strada Col Alt, 105, 39033 Corvara in Badia BZ, Italy
Uniqueness: Located in Hotel La Perla, this Michelin-starred restaurant features a cozy, rustic atmosphere with wood-paneled walls. The menu combines traditional Ladin dishes with modern twists, using high-quality local ingredients.

3. **Restaurant Terra**

Location: Sarentino
Address: Località Casateia, 51, 39058 Sarentino BZ, Italy
Uniqueness: Awarded two Michelin stars, Terra offers a unique dining experience in a remote mountain setting. Chef Heinrich Schneider creates innovative dishes that reflect the natural surroundings, with a strong emphasis on foraged ingredients.

4. Tilia

Location: Dobbiaco
Address: Via Dolomiti, 31, 39034 Dobbiaco BZ, Italy
Uniqueness: A Michelin-starred restaurant known for its intimate setting and creative cuisine. Chef Chris Oberhammer crafts contemporary dishes that blend traditional South Tyrolean flavors with international influences.

5. El Molin

Location: Cavalese
Address: Via Giuseppe Verdi, 6, 38033 Cavalese TN, Italy
Uniqueness: Housed in a historic 17th-century mill, this Michelin-starred restaurant offers a rustic yet elegant dining experience. Chef Alessandro Gilmozzi is known for his avant-garde approach to traditional Trentino dishes, incorporating local herbs and foraged ingredients.

6. Osteria Tyrol

Location: Ortisei
Address: Via Rezia, 19, 39046 Ortisei BZ, Italy
Uniqueness: A charming restaurant that serves traditional South Tyrolean cuisine in a warm, wood-paneled setting. The menu features hearty dishes such as speck, dumplings, and game meats, paired with an excellent selection of local wines.

7. Restaurant Malga Panna

Location: Moena
Address: Strada de Sort, 64, 38035 Moena TN, Italy
Uniqueness: Nestled in the mountains, this Michelin-starred restaurant offers stunning views and a tranquil atmosphere. Chef Paolo Donei creates exquisite dishes that highlight the flavors of the Dolomites, using seasonal and local ingredients.

8. Anna Stuben

Location: Ortisei
Address: Via Rezia, 7, 39046 Ortisei BZ, Italy

Uniqueness: Located in the ADLER Spa Resort Dolomiti, this Michelin-starred restaurant combines elegant dining with a focus on local and organic produce. Chef Reimund Brunner crafts sophisticated dishes that showcase the best of South Tyrolean cuisine.

9. **Jora Mountain Dining**

   Location: San Candido
   Address: Haunoldweg, 8, 39038 San Candido BZ, Italy
   Uniqueness: A unique dining experience set in the mountains, offering breathtaking views and a cozy, rustic ambiance. The menu features creative dishes made with locally sourced ingredients, highlighting the flavors of the region.

10. **Rifugio Fuciade**

    Location: Passo San Pellegrino
    Address: Località Fuciade, 38035 Soraga TN, Italy
    Uniqueness: A mountain refuge renowned for its delicious cuisine and charming setting. Accessible via a scenic hike or snowshoeing in

winter, Rifugio Fuciade serves traditional Ladin dishes and homemade desserts, offering a true taste of the Dolomites.

These top restaurants in the Dolomites provide a diverse range of culinary experiences, from traditional South Tyrolean fare to innovative, Michelin-starred creations. Each restaurant offers a unique setting and exceptional food, making them must-visit destinations for any food lover exploring the Dolomites.

Culture and Traditions

The Dolomites are a region rich in cultural heritage and traditions, shaped by the diverse communities that have lived here for centuries. The unique blend of Italian, German, and Ladin influences is evident in the architecture, language, festivals, and daily life of the people. This cultural mosaic creates a vibrant and fascinating atmosphere that adds depth to the natural beauty of the Dolomites.

Language

The Dolomites are home to three main linguistic groups: Italian, German, and Ladin. This trilingualism reflects the region's complex history and cultural diversity.

> Italian: The majority language, spoken widely throughout the region, especially in larger towns and cities.

German: Predominantly spoken in South Tyrol and certain parts of Trentino. This reflects the historical ties to the Austro-Hungarian Empire.

Ladin: An ancient Romance language spoken in several valleys, including Val Gardena, Val Badia, and Val di Fassa. Efforts are made to preserve this unique linguistic heritage, with Ladin taught in schools and used in local media.

Architecture

The architectural style in the Dolomites varies, reflecting the region's cultural diversity and historical influences.

Tyrolean Architecture: Characterized by wooden chalets with steeply pitched roofs, intricate woodwork, and balconies adorned with flowers. This style is common in South Tyrol and other German-speaking areas.

Ladin Architecture: Features stone and wood construction with distinctive sgraffito decorations, which are artistic designs scratched into the plaster of buildings.

Italian Influence: More prominent in urban areas, with Renaissance and Baroque elements visible in churches, public buildings, and town squares.

Festivals and Celebrations

The Dolomites host numerous festivals and events throughout the year, celebrating everything from religious holidays to local customs and agricultural traditions.

Christmas Markets: During December, towns like Bolzano, Bressanone, and Brunico transform into festive wonderlands with markets selling crafts, food, and mulled wine.
Easter Processions: These traditional religious events often feature elaborate parades with participants in historical costumes.
Sagra di San Lorenzo: A popular festival in August, celebrated in various Ladin valleys with music, dancing, and local food.
Törggelen: An autumn tradition in South Tyrol where people gather to taste the new wine from

the harvest, accompanied by roasted chestnuts and hearty Tyrolean dishes.

Cortina Fashion Week: Held in the chic town of Cortina d'Ampezzo, this event showcases high-end fashion and local designers, blending modern trends with traditional styles.

Cuisine

The culinary traditions of the Dolomites are a reflection of the region's cultural diversity, offering a delicious blend of Italian, German, and Ladin influences.

Speck: A type of smoked ham that is a staple in South Tyrolean cuisine. It is often enjoyed with bread, cheese, and pickles.
Canederli: Large bread dumplings mixed with various ingredients like cheese, spinach, or speck, served in broth or with butter and sage.
Polenta: A versatile cornmeal dish, typically served with meat stews or mushrooms.
Strudel: A popular dessert, especially apple strudel, featuring layers of flaky pastry filled with spiced apples.

Casunziei: A type of Ladin pasta, often filled with red beets and served with melted butter and poppy seeds.

Traditional Attire

Traditional clothing is an important part of the cultural identity in the Dolomites, particularly during festivals and special occasions.

Dirndl and Lederhosen: Traditional Tyrolean attire for women and men, respectively. Dirndls are dresses with fitted bodices and full skirts, while lederhosen are leather shorts or trousers.
Ladin Costumes: Feature elaborate embroidery and bright colors, with specific designs varying between valleys. Women's costumes often include a richly decorated apron and headdress.

Folklore and Legends

The Dolomites are steeped in folklore and legends, with many stories passed down through generations.

King Laurin and the Rosengarten: One of the most famous legends tells of King Laurin, a dwarf king whose rose garden was transformed into stone, creating the Rosengarten mountain range. According to legend, the roses can still be seen glowing red at sunset.

Dolomite Witches: Tales of witches and supernatural beings are common in local folklore, adding a mystical element to the region's cultural narrative.

Arts and Crafts

Traditional arts and crafts are an integral part of Dolomite culture, reflecting the region's history and natural environment.

Woodcarving: A highly respected craft, especially in Val Gardena, where artisans create intricate sculptures, religious figures, and decorative items.

Ladin Textiles: Handwoven fabrics and lacework are traditional crafts in Ladin valleys, often featuring patterns inspired by nature.

Pottery and Ceramics: Local artisans produce beautifully crafted pottery and ceramics, often decorated with motifs inspired by the Dolomites.

Conclusion

The culture and traditions of the Dolomites are as captivating as the landscapes themselves. The region's unique blend of languages, architecture, festivals, cuisine, and folklore offers visitors a rich and immersive cultural experience. Exploring the cultural heritage of the Dolomites enhances any visit, providing a deeper understanding and appreciation of this extraordinary region.

Flora and Fauna of the Dolomites.

The Dolomites, with their diverse altitudes and climates, boast a rich and varied tapestry of flora and fauna. This unique region supports a wide range of plant and animal life, making it a paradise for nature lovers and outdoor enthusiasts. Here's a detailed look at the flora and fauna you can encounter in the Dolomites.

Flora

The plant life in the Dolomites changes dramatically with altitude, from lush forests in the valleys to hardy alpine plants in the high-altitude meadows.

1. Forests:

> Common Tree Species: The lower altitudes (up to about 1,500 meters or 4,921 feet) are dominated by dense forests of Norway spruce, European larch, and Scots pine. Higher up, you'll find Swiss stone pine and dwarf pine.

Subalpine Zone: In the subalpine zone (1,500 to 2,200 meters or 4,921 to 7,218 feet), you'll encounter more mixed forests with species like silver fir and beech.

2. Alpine Meadows:

Alpine Flowers: Above the tree line, the landscape transforms into alpine meadows filled with vibrant wildflowers during the summer months. Common species include gentian, edelweiss, alpine aster, and various orchids.
Grasslands: These meadows are rich in grasses and low shrubs like rhododendrons, which provide stunning displays of color.

3. Rock and Scree Habitats:

Specialized Plants: In the highest altitudes, where only the toughest plants can survive, you'll find species adapted to extreme conditions, such as saxifrages, moss campion, and cushion plants that form low, dense mats to withstand the harsh weather.

4. Wetlands and Water Bodies:

Lakes and Streams: The clear waters of alpine lakes and streams support a variety of aquatic plants, including water lilies and pondweeds.
Marshes and Bogs: In wetter areas, you'll find bogs and marshes with plants like cotton grass, sundew, and bog rosemary.

Fauna

The diverse habitats of the Dolomites provide a home to a wide array of wildlife, from large mammals to small insects.

1. Mammals:

Chamois (Rupicapra rupicapra): Agile and sure-footed, these goat-antelopes are commonly seen in rocky areas and steep slopes.

Marmots (Marmota marmota): These large, burrowing rodents are a familiar sight in alpine meadows. Their loud whistles can often be heard echoing through the valleys.

Red Deer (Cervus elaphus): The largest deer species in the region, often spotted in forested areas during dawn and dusk.

Roe Deer (Capreolus capreolus): Smaller than red deer, they are common in mixed woodlands and clearings.

Ibex (Capra ibex): Once nearly extinct, these impressive mountain goats with large, curved horns have made a comeback and can be seen in high-altitude rocky areas.

2. Birds:

Golden Eagle (Aquila chrysaetos): The majestic golden eagle soars above the peaks, hunting for small mammals and birds.

Alpine Chough (Pyrrhocorax graculus): These black birds with yellow beaks are often seen performing acrobatic flight displays near cliffs.

Ptarmigan (Lagopus muta): This grouse species changes plumage with the seasons, blending into snowy winter landscapes or rocky summer terrain.

Bearded Vulture (Gypaetus barbatus): A rare sight, this large vulture is known for its impressive wingspan and unique habit of dropping bones to break them open.

3. Reptiles and Amphibians:

European Adder (Vipera berus): A venomous snake found in a variety of habitats, from forests to alpine meadows.

Common Frog (Rana temporaria): Frequently found near water bodies, these amphibians are common throughout the Dolomites.

Alpine Salamander (Salamandra atra): Typically found in moist, shaded areas, this species is adapted to cooler climates.

4. Insects and Invertebrates:

Butterflies and Moths: The Dolomites are home to a stunning variety of butterflies, including the Apollo (Parnassius apollo) and the Small Tortoiseshell (Aglais urticae).
Beetles and Bugs: Numerous beetle species, including the Alpine longhorn beetle (Rosalia alpina), can be found in forested areas and meadows.
Spiders and Insects: Various species of spiders, ants, and other insects play crucial roles in the ecosystem, from pollination to decomposition.

Conservation Efforts

The unique biodiversity of the Dolomites is protected through various conservation efforts. Several areas are designated as nature reserves and national parks, such as the Parco Naturale Paneveggio – Pale di San Martino and the Parco Naturale Dolomiti d'Ampezzo. These protected areas ensure the preservation of habitats and species, allowing future generations to enjoy the natural beauty and ecological richness of the Dolomites.

Conclusion

The flora and fauna of the Dolomites are as diverse and spectacular as the landscapes themselves. From the vibrant alpine meadows to the dense forests and high-altitude rocky habitats, the region supports an incredible array of plant and animal life. Exploring the Dolomites offers a unique opportunity to witness this biodiversity firsthand, whether you are hiking through wildflower-strewn meadows, spotting marmots and chamois, or marveling at the sight of a golden eagle soaring overhead.

The Walks

Walk 1: Lago di Braies

Highlights

Scenic Beauty: Crystal-clear lake surrounded by the dramatic peaks of the Dolomites.
Photogenic Spots: Iconic wooden boathouse and pier.
Family-Friendly: Easy trail suitable for all ages.

Route Description

Starting Point: Lago di Braies parking lot.
Distance: Approximately 4 km (2.5 miles).
Duration: 1.5 to 2 hours.

Route: Begin at the northern shore, follow the well-marked path around the lake clockwise. The trail is mostly flat with a few gentle inclines and offers continuous stunning views of the lake and surrounding mountains.

Tips and Recommendations

Best Time to Visit: Early morning or late afternoon to avoid crowds.
Gear: Comfortable walking shoes, water, and a camera.
Additional Activities: Rent a rowboat or enjoy a picnic by the lake.
Safety: Stay on the marked path and be cautious near the water's edge.

This walk is perfect for soaking in the beauty of the Dolomites while enjoying a leisurely stroll around one of its most picturesque lakes.

Walk 2: Rifugio Biella Loop

Highlights

Mountain Scenery: Panoramic views of the Dolomites.
Wildlife Spotting: Opportunity to see marmots and chamois.
Rifugio Experience: Visit Rifugio Biella for a rest and refreshments.

Route Description

Starting Point: Malga Ra Stua parking area.
Distance: Approximately 10 km (6.2 miles).
Duration: 4 to 5 hours.
Route: From Malga Ra Stua, follow the trail towards Rifugio Sennes. Continue to Rifugio Biella, enjoying the views of Croda del Becco. Loop back via a different path that reconnects with the initial trail.

Tips and Recommendations

Best Time to Visit: Late spring to early autumn for best trail conditions.

Gear: Sturdy hiking boots, layered clothing, water, and snacks.

Additional Activities: Enjoy a meal at Rifugio Biella and take in the surrounding views.

Safety: Check weather forecasts and trail conditions before setting out. Carry a map or GPS.

Walk 3: Monte Specie

Highlights

- **Panoramic Views:** Breathtaking vistas of the Tre Cime di Lavaredo and surrounding peaks.
- **Scenic Landscape:** Alpine meadows and lush forests.
- **Historical Interest:** World War I fortifications along the route.

Route Description

- **Starting Point:** Prato Piazza parking area.
- **Distance:** Approximately 8 km (5 miles) round trip.
- **Duration:** 3 to 4 hours.
- **Route:** Begin at Prato Piazza, following the marked trail towards the summit of Monte Specie. The path is moderately steep but well-maintained. Once at the top, enjoy the 360-degree views before descending the same way.

Tips and Recommendations

- **Best Time to Visit:** Late spring to early autumn for clear paths and good weather.
- **Gear:** Sturdy hiking boots, layered clothing, sun protection, water, and snacks.
- **Additional Activities:** Visit the nearby Prato Piazza plateau for additional walking trails and scenic views.
- **Safety:** Be prepared for sudden weather changes and ensure you have a map or GPS device.

This walk provides stunning panoramic views and a moderate hiking challenge, making it a rewarding experience for those exploring the Dolomites.

Walk 4: Alpe di Sennes Circuit

Highlights

- **Stunning Landscapes:** Expansive alpine meadows and dramatic mountain backdrops.
- **Wildlife:** Possible sightings of chamois and marmots.
- **Rifugios:** Several mountain huts offering refreshments and local cuisine.

Route Description

- **Starting Point:** Pederü parking area.
- **Distance:** Approximately 14 km (8.7 miles).
- **Duration:** 5 to 6 hours.
- **Route:** From Pederü, follow the trail to Rifugio Fodara Vedla. Continue towards Rifugio Sennes, then loop back towards Rifugio Pederü via a different path. The trail is well-marked and offers varied terrain, including meadows, rocky paths, and forested areas.

Tips and Recommendations

- **Best Time to Visit:** Late spring to early autumn for the best trail conditions and open rifugios.

- **Gear:** Sturdy hiking boots, layered clothing, sun protection, water, and snacks.
- **Additional Activities:** Stop at the rifugios for a meal or drink, and take in the breathtaking views.
- **Safety:** Check the weather forecast and trail conditions before starting. Carry a map or GPS device.

Walk 5: Landro to Cortina on the Old Railway Line

Highlights

- **Historical Route:** Follow the path of the old Dolomites railway, rich in history.
- **Scenic Views:** Stunning views of the Dolomite peaks and lush valleys.
- **Cultural Landmarks:** Pass by old railway stations and tunnels.

Route Description

- **Starting Point:** Landro (Dürrensee) parking area.
- **Distance:** Approximately 16 km (10 miles).
- **Duration:** 5 to 6 hours.
- **Route:** Start at Landro and follow the well-marked trail along the former railway line towards Cortina d'Ampezzo. The route is mostly flat with gentle inclines, passing through tunnels and old stations, and

offering panoramic views of the surrounding mountains.

Tips and Recommendations

- **Best Time to Visit:** Late spring to early autumn for pleasant weather and clear paths.
- **Gear:** Comfortable walking shoes, layered clothing, sun protection, water, and snacks.
- **Additional Activities:** Bring a camera to capture the scenic views and historical landmarks along the way.
- **Safety:** Ensure you have a map or GPS device. Check the weather forecast before heading out.

This walk provides a unique blend of history and natural beauty, making it an enjoyable and educational hike for those exploring the Dolomites.

Walk 6: Torre dei Scarperi Circuit

Highlights

- **Dramatic Scenery:** Towering rock formations and expansive alpine views.
- **Wildlife:** Opportunities to see marmots and alpine ibex.

- **Mountain Hut:** Visit Rifugio Tre Scarperi for a break and refreshments.

Route Description

- **Starting Point:** Val Fiscalina parking area.
- **Distance:** Approximately 12 km (7.5 miles).
- **Duration:** 5 to 6 hours.
- **Route:** Begin at the Val Fiscalina parking area and follow the trail towards Rifugio Tre Scarperi. From there, continue along the circuit path that loops around the Torre dei Scarperi, passing through meadows and rocky landscapes before returning to the starting point.

Tips and Recommendations

- **Best Time to Visit:** Late spring to early autumn for optimal trail conditions.
- **Gear:** Sturdy hiking boots, layered clothing, sun protection, water, and snacks.
- **Additional Activities:** Stop at Rifugio Tre Scarperi for a meal and enjoy the stunning views.
- **Safety:** Be prepared for sudden weather changes, carry a map or GPS, and check trail conditions before starting.

This circuit offers a challenging yet rewarding hike with spectacular views and the chance to experience the rugged beauty of the Dolomites up close.

Walk 7: The Val Fiscalina Tour

Highlights

- **Breathtaking Valley Views:** Beautiful scenery with lush meadows, dense forests, and towering peaks.
- **Peaceful Atmosphere:** A tranquil hike through one of the quieter areas of the Dolomites.
- **Cultural Interest:** Historic wooden barns and traditional alpine architecture.

Route Description

- **Starting Point:** Val Fiscalina parking area (Fischleintal).
- **Distance:** Approximately 10 km (6.2 miles).
- **Duration:** 3 to 4 hours.
- **Route:** Start from the Val Fiscalina parking area and follow the well-marked trail through the valley. The path is relatively flat and easy, winding through picturesque meadows and forests. The trail loops back to the starting point, offering continuous views of the surrounding mountains.

Tips and Recommendations

- **Best Time to Visit:** Late spring to early autumn for the best weather and trail conditions.

- **Gear:** Comfortable walking shoes, layered clothing, sun protection, water, and snacks.
- **Additional Activities:** Enjoy a picnic in one of the meadows or visit a nearby mountain hut for local cuisine.
- **Safety:** Check the weather forecast and trail conditions before heading out. Carry a map or GPS for navigation.

Walk 8: The Tre Cime di Lavaredo Loop

Highlights

- **Iconic Peaks:** Stunning views of the Tre Cime di Lavaredo, one of the most famous landmarks in the Dolomites.
- **Alpine Scenery:** Dramatic landscapes featuring rugged peaks, alpine meadows, and pristine lakes.
- **Historical Interest:** World War I tunnels and fortifications along the route.

Route Description

- **Starting Point:** Rifugio Auronzo parking area.
- **Distance:** Approximately 10 km (6.2 miles).
- **Duration:** 4 to 5 hours.
- **Route:** Begin at Rifugio Auronzo and follow the well-marked trail towards Rifugio Lavaredo. Continue to Forcella Lavaredo for a panoramic view

of the Tre Cime. From there, the trail loops around the peaks, passing Rifugio Locatelli. The path offers a mix of gentle slopes and steeper sections, with several spots to rest and take in the scenery before returning to Rifugio Auronzo.

Tips and Recommendations

- **Best Time to Visit:** Late spring to early autumn for clear trails and optimal weather.
- **Gear:** Sturdy hiking boots, layered clothing, sun protection, water, and snacks.
- **Additional Activities:** Explore the World War I tunnels and take plenty of photos at the various viewpoints.
- **Safety:** Be prepared for sudden weather changes, carry a map or GPS, and check trail conditions before starting.

The Tre Cime di Lavaredo Loop offers an unforgettable hike with some of the most iconic views in the Dolomites, making it a must-do for any visitor to the region.

Walk 9: Through the Cadini di Misurina

Highlights

- **Spectacular Peaks:** Dramatic spires and pinnacles of the Cadini di Misurina range.

- **Panoramic Views:** Breathtaking vistas of the surrounding Dolomites, including the Tre Cime di Lavaredo.
- **Tranquil Trails:** Less crowded paths offering a serene hiking experience.

Route Description

- **Starting Point:** Rifugio Auronzo parking area.
- **Distance:** Approximately 12 km (7.5 miles).
- **Duration:** 5 to 6 hours.
- **Route:** Start from Rifugio Auronzo and follow the trail towards Forcella del Diavolo. The path winds through rocky terrain and alpine meadows, offering stunning views of the Cadini di Misurina. Continue to Forcella del Nevaio, then loop back to the starting point via a different route, enjoying panoramic views throughout the hike.

Tips and Recommendations

- **Best Time to Visit:** Late spring to early autumn for the best weather and trail conditions.
- **Gear:** Sturdy hiking boots, layered clothing, sun protection, water, and snacks.
- **Additional Activities:** Take time to explore the various viewpoints and capture photos of the unique rock formations.
- **Safety:** Be prepared for sudden weather changes, carry a map or GPS, and ensure you have enough provisions for a full day hike.

Walking through the Cadini di Misurina offers a challenging yet rewarding experience with some of the most dramatic scenery in the Dolomites, perfect for avid hikers seeking a less crowded trail.

Walk 10: Monte Piana

Highlights

- **Historical Significance:** Site of intense World War I battles, with remnants of trenches and fortifications.
- **Panoramic Views:** Stunning vistas of the surrounding Dolomite peaks and valleys.
- **Unique Landscape:** Mix of open meadows, rocky outcrops, and historical sites.

Route Description

- **Starting Point:** Misurina parking area.
- **Distance:** Approximately 8 km (5 miles).
- **Duration:** 3 to 4 hours.
- **Route:** Begin at the Misurina parking area and follow the marked trail up to Monte Piana. The trail ascends

gradually through meadows and forested areas, leading to the plateau at the top. Explore the World War I trenches and fortifications while taking in the panoramic views. Descend back to Misurina via the same route.

Tips and Recommendations

- **Best Time to Visit:** Late spring to early autumn for optimal weather and trail conditions.
- **Gear:** Sturdy hiking boots, layered clothing, sun protection, water, and snacks.
- **Additional Activities:** Visit the open-air museum on Monte Piana to learn more about its historical significance.
- **Safety:** Be prepared for sudden weather changes, carry a map or GPS, and respect the historical sites by not disturbing the remnants.

Monte Piana offers a unique blend of natural beauty and historical significance, making it a compelling destination for hikers and history enthusiasts alike.

Walk 11: Lago di Misurina

Highlights

- **Scenic Lake:** Beautiful views of the crystal-clear Lago di Misurina surrounded by majestic peaks.

- **Family-Friendly:** Easy, flat walk suitable for all ages.
- **Cultural Interest:** Close proximity to historical hotels and the famous Misurina Sanatorium.

Route Description

- **Starting Point:** Lago di Misurina parking area.
- **Distance:** Approximately 4 km (2.5 miles) round trip.
- **Duration:** 1 to 1.5 hours.
- **Route:** Start from the Lago di Misurina parking area and follow the well-marked path that encircles the lake. The trail is mostly flat and easy to navigate, providing continuous views of the lake and surrounding mountains. The path is suitable for a leisurely stroll, offering plenty of spots to stop and enjoy the scenery.

Tips and Recommendations

- **Best Time to Visit:** Spring to autumn for pleasant weather and clear views.
- **Gear:** Comfortable walking shoes, sun protection, water, and a camera.
- **Additional Activities:** Enjoy a picnic by the lake, rent a paddleboat, or visit the nearby Misurina Sanatorium.
- **Safety:** The trail is straightforward, but always check the weather forecast before heading out.

Walk 12: Val Popena Alta

Highlights

- **Secluded Valley:** Quiet and less frequented trail offering solitude and natural beauty.
- **Diverse Scenery:** Mix of dense forests, alpine meadows, and rocky landscapes.
- **Mountain Views:** Panoramic vistas of the surrounding Dolomite peaks.

Route Description

- **Starting Point:** Lake Antorno parking area.
- **Distance:** Approximately 8 km (5 miles) round trip.
- **Duration:** 3 to 4 hours.
- **Route:** Start at the Lake Antorno parking area and follow the trail into Val Popena Alta. The path gradually ascends through forests and meadows, eventually opening up to stunning views of the surrounding mountains. The trail is well-marked and offers a moderate hike with some rocky sections. Return via the same route.

Tips and Recommendations

- **Best Time to Visit:** Late spring to early autumn for the best weather and trail conditions.
- **Gear:** Sturdy hiking boots, layered clothing, sun protection, water, and snacks.

- **Additional Activities:** Enjoy a picnic in one of the meadows or explore the area around Lake Antorno.
- **Safety:** Check weather forecasts before setting out, carry a map or GPS, and be prepared for sudden weather changes.

Val Popena Alta offers a peaceful and scenic hike through diverse landscapes, making it an excellent choice for those seeking tranquility and natural beauty in the Dolomites.

Walk 13: Rifugio Vandelli Traverse

Highlights

- **Alpine Scenery:** Stunning views of Sorapiss Lake and surrounding peaks.
- **Rifugio Experience:** Enjoy a stop at Rifugio Vandelli for refreshments.
- **Varied Terrain:** Diverse landscapes including forests, rocky paths, and meadows.

Route Description

- **Starting Point:** Passo Tre Croci parking area.
- **Distance:** Approximately 12 km (7.5 miles) round trip.
- **Duration:** 5 to 6 hours.
- **Route:** Begin at the Passo Tre Croci parking area and follow trail no. 215 towards Rifugio Vandelli. The trail ascends gradually through forests and rocky

sections, offering glimpses of the stunning Sorapiss Lake. Continue to Rifugio Vandelli, where you can rest and enjoy the scenery. After a break, retrace your steps back to the starting point.

Tips and Recommendations

- **Best Time to Visit:** Late spring to early autumn for optimal trail conditions and open rifugios.
- **Gear:** Sturdy hiking boots, layered clothing, sun protection, water, and snacks.
- **Additional Activities:** Take a detour to Sorapiss Lake for breathtaking views and photo opportunities.
- **Safety:** Be prepared for sudden weather changes, carry a map or GPS, and ensure you have enough provisions for the entire hike.

The Rifugio Vandelli Traverse offers a rewarding hike with varied terrain and the opportunity to experience the beauty and hospitality of the Dolomites.

Walk 14: Forcella Zumèles and the Cristallo

Highlights

- **Breathtaking Views:** Panoramic vistas of the Cristallo group and surrounding peaks.
- **Diverse Terrain:** Mix of forest paths, rocky sections, and high alpine meadows.

- **Historical Interest:** Remnants of World War I fortifications.

Route Description

- **Starting Point:** Rio Gere parking area.
- **Distance:** Approximately 10 km (6.2 miles) round trip.
- **Duration:** 5 to 6 hours.
- **Route:** Begin at the Rio Gere parking area and follow trail no. 203 towards Forcella Zumèles. The path ascends through forests and rocky terrain, offering stunning views of the Cristallo massif. Continue to Forcella Zumèles, where you can take in the panoramic views and explore the historical sites. Return via the same trail to the starting point.

Tips and Recommendations

- **Best Time to Visit:** Late spring to early autumn for the best weather and trail conditions.
- **Gear:** Sturdy hiking boots, layered clothing, sun protection, water, and snacks.
- **Additional Activities:** Take time to explore the World War I fortifications and enjoy a picnic with a view.
- **Safety:** Check weather forecasts before setting out, carry a map or GPS, and be prepared for sudden weather changes.

The hike to Forcella Zumèles and the Cristallo offers a challenging yet rewarding experience with breathtaking views and a touch of history, perfect for avid hikers and history enthusiasts.

Walk 15: Below the Antelao

Highlights

- **Majestic Views:** Stunning vistas of Mount Antelao, known as the "King of the Dolomites."
- **Diverse Landscapes:** A mix of dense forests, alpine meadows, and rocky terrains.
- **Quiet Trails:** Less frequented paths offering tranquility and solitude.

Route Description

- **Starting Point:** San Vito di Cadore parking area.
- **Distance:** Approximately 12 km (7.5 miles) round trip.
- **Duration:** 5 to 6 hours.
- **Route:** Begin at the San Vito di Cadore parking area and follow trail no. 250 towards Rifugio Scotter-Palatini. Continue along the path below Mount Antelao, enjoying the varied landscapes and panoramic views. The trail loops back towards San Vito di Cadore, passing through beautiful meadows and forested areas.

Tips and Recommendations

- **Best Time to Visit:** Late spring to early autumn for the best weather and trail conditions.
- **Gear:** Sturdy hiking boots, layered clothing, sun protection, water, and snacks.
- **Additional Activities:** Stop at Rifugio Scotter-Palatini for a meal or refreshments and enjoy the view.
- **Safety:** Be prepared for sudden weather changes, carry a map or GPS, and ensure you have enough provisions for the entire hike.

Walk 16: Rifugio Padova and Rifugio Tita Barba

Highlights

- **Rifugio Experience:** Enjoy local cuisine and hospitality at two charming mountain huts.
- **Scenic Beauty:** Diverse landscapes including forests, meadows, and rocky outcrops.
- **Panoramic Views:** Stunning vistas of the surrounding Dolomite peaks.

Route Description

- **Starting Point:** Rifugio Padova parking area.
- **Distance:** Approximately 10 km (6.2 miles) round trip.
- **Duration:** 4 to 5 hours.

- **Route:** Start at the Rifugio Padova parking area and follow the trail towards Rifugio Padova. Continue on the well-marked path to Rifugio Tita Barba. The trail offers a mix of forested sections, open meadows, and rocky terrain, providing beautiful views throughout the hike. After enjoying a meal or refreshments at Rifugio Tita Barba, return via the same route to the starting point.

Tips and Recommendations

- **Best Time to Visit:** Late spring to early autumn for optimal trail conditions and open rifugios.
- **Gear:** Sturdy hiking boots, layered clothing, sun protection, water, and snacks.
- **Additional Activities:** Take time to relax and enjoy the hospitality at both rifugios, and capture photos of the stunning landscapes.
- **Safety:** Check weather forecasts before setting out, carry a map or GPS, and be prepared for sudden weather changes.

Walk 17: The Pramper Circuit

Highlights

- **Diverse Scenery:** Experience a variety of landscapes, including lush forests, alpine meadows, and rugged mountain terrain.

- **Rifugio Experience:** Stop at Rifugio Pramperet for refreshments and stunning views.
- **Wildlife:** Opportunities to spot local wildlife such as marmots and chamois.

Route Description

- **Starting Point:** Pian de la Fopa parking area.
- **Distance:** Approximately 14 km (8.7 miles) round trip.
- **Duration:** 5 to 6 hours.
- **Route:** Start from the Pian de la Fopa parking area and follow trail no. 523 towards Rifugio Sommariva al Pramperet. The trail ascends gradually through dense forests and opens up to alpine meadows. Continue along the circuit, passing Rifugio Pramperet where you can take a break and enjoy the panoramic views. The trail loops back through diverse terrain, returning to the starting point.

Tips and Recommendations

- **Best Time to Visit:** Late spring to early autumn for favorable weather and open rifugios.
- **Gear:** Sturdy hiking boots, layered clothing, sun protection, water, and snacks.
- **Additional Activities:** Enjoy a meal or refreshments at Rifugio Pramperet and take in the surrounding views.

- **Safety:** Check weather forecasts before setting out, carry a map or GPS, and be prepared for sudden weather changes.

The Pramper Circuit offers a rewarding hike with diverse scenery, wildlife spotting opportunities, and the chance to experience the warm hospitality of a Dolomite rifugio.

Walk 18: Lago Coldai and the Civetta

Highlights

- **Stunning Alpine Lake:** Beautiful Lago Coldai with crystal-clear waters and breathtaking mountain reflections.
- **Impressive Peaks:** Close-up views of the Civetta massif, one of the most striking mountains in the Dolomites.
- **Varied Terrain:** A mix of meadows, rocky paths, and high-altitude trails.

Route Description

- **Starting Point:** Alleghe parking area (Piani di Pezzè).
- **Distance:** Approximately 12 km (7.5 miles) round trip.
- **Duration:** 5 to 6 hours.

- **Route:** Start from the Piani di Pezzè parking area and take the cable car to Col dei Baldi. From there, follow trail no. 556 towards Lago Coldai. The path ascends gradually through alpine meadows and rocky sections, offering stunning views of the surrounding peaks. Once at Lago Coldai, take time to enjoy the scenery and explore the area around the lake. Continue towards Rifugio Coldai for a rest and refreshments before returning via the same route.

Tips and Recommendations

- **Best Time to Visit:** Late spring to early autumn for clear trails and optimal weather.
- **Gear:** Sturdy hiking boots, layered clothing, sun protection, water, and snacks.
- **Additional Activities:** Explore the area around Lago Coldai and take photos of the stunning landscape. Enjoy a meal or drink at Rifugio Coldai.
- **Safety:** Check weather forecasts before setting out, carry a map or GPS, and be prepared for sudden weather changes.

Walk 19: The Pelmo Tour

Highlights

- **Iconic Mountain:** Close-up views of Mount Pelmo, known as the "Throne of the Gods."

- **Diverse Landscapes:** Varied terrain including forests, alpine meadows, and rocky paths.
- **Panoramic Vistas:** Stunning 360-degree views of the surrounding Dolomite peaks.

Route Description

- **Starting Point:** Passo Staulanza parking area.
- **Distance:** Approximately 14 km (8.7 miles) round trip.
- **Duration:** 6 to 7 hours.
- **Route:** Begin at the Passo Staulanza parking area and follow trail no. 472 towards Rifugio Venezia. The trail ascends through dense forests and open meadows, providing beautiful views of Mount Pelmo. Continue around the base of Pelmo, following the marked path that loops back towards the starting point. The trail offers varied terrain, including some rocky sections and high-altitude paths.

Tips and Recommendations

- **Best Time to Visit:** Late spring to early autumn for optimal trail conditions and weather.
- **Gear:** Sturdy hiking boots, layered clothing, sun protection, water, and snacks.
- **Additional Activities:** Stop at Rifugio Venezia for a meal or refreshments and enjoy the panoramic views.
- **Safety:** Check weather forecasts before setting out, carry a map or GPS, and be prepared for sudden weather changes.

The Pelmo Tour offers a challenging yet rewarding hike with diverse landscapes and breathtaking views, making it an unforgettable experience for hikers exploring the Dolomites.

Walk 20: Gores de Federa

Highlights

- **Scenic Waterfalls:** Series of beautiful waterfalls along the trail.
- **Lush Forests:** Dense, verdant forests providing shade and a tranquil atmosphere.
- **Panoramic Views:** Stunning views of the Dolomite peaks and valleys.

Route Description

- **Starting Point:** Lago Pianozes parking area.
- **Distance:** Approximately 8 km (5 miles) round trip.
- **Duration:** 3 to 4 hours.
- **Route:** Start at the Lago Pianozes parking area and follow the trail marked for Gores de Federa. The path winds through lush forests and along a series of picturesque waterfalls. The trail includes some moderate ascents and descents, offering various vantage points for enjoying the waterfalls and panoramic views. The route loops back to the starting point, passing through meadows and forested areas.

Tips and Recommendations

- **Best Time to Visit:** Late spring to early autumn for the best weather and trail conditions.
- **Gear:** Comfortable hiking shoes, layered clothing, sun protection, water, and snacks.
- **Additional Activities:** Enjoy a picnic at one of the scenic spots along the trail and take plenty of photos of the waterfalls.
- **Safety:** Check weather forecasts before setting out, carry a map or GPS, and be cautious on slippery sections near the waterfalls.

Walk 21: Around the Croda da Lago

Highlights

- **Scenic Loop:** Complete circuit around the impressive Croda da Lago massif.
- **Alpine Lakes:** Beautiful views of Lago Federa.
- **Varied Terrain:** A mix of meadows, forests, and rocky paths.

Route Description

- **Starting Point:** Passo Giau parking area.
- **Distance:** Approximately 13 km (8 miles) round trip.
- **Duration:** 5 to 6 hours.
- **Route:** Begin at the Passo Giau parking area and follow trail no. 436 towards Rifugio Croda da Lago. The path ascends through forests and meadows,

reaching the stunning Lago Federa. Continue around the Croda da Lago massif, enjoying panoramic views of the Dolomite peaks. The trail loops back to the starting point, offering varied terrain and beautiful scenery throughout the hike.

Tips and Recommendations

- **Best Time to Visit:** Late spring to early autumn for optimal weather and trail conditions.
- **Gear:** Sturdy hiking boots, layered clothing, sun protection, water, and snacks.
- **Additional Activities:** Stop at Rifugio Croda da Lago for a meal or refreshments and take in the views of Lago Federa.
- **Safety:** Check weather forecasts before setting out, carry a map or GPS, and be prepared for sudden weather changes.

The hike around the Croda da Lago offers a rewarding loop with diverse landscapes and stunning views, making it a must-do for hikers exploring the Dolomites.

Walk 22: The Cinque Torri

Highlights

- **Iconic Rock Formations:** Explore the famous Cinque Torri (Five Towers) rock formations.

- **Historical Interest:** Visit World War I trenches and fortifications.
- **Panoramic Views:** Stunning vistas of the surrounding Dolomite peaks.

Route Description

- **Starting Point:** Rifugio Bai de Dones parking area.
- **Distance:** Approximately 9 km (5.6 miles) round trip.
- **Duration:** 3 to 4 hours.
- **Route:** Start at the Rifugio Bai de Dones parking area and take the cable car to Rifugio Scoiattoli (optional). Follow trail no. 439 towards the Cinque Torri. The path winds through alpine meadows and rocky areas, offering close-up views of the impressive rock formations. Continue to Rifugio Cinque Torri for a break, then explore the World War I trenches and fortifications. Loop back to the starting point, enjoying panoramic views throughout the hike.

Tips and Recommendations

- **Best Time to Visit:** Late spring to early autumn for the best weather and trail conditions.
- **Gear:** Sturdy hiking boots, layered clothing, sun protection, water, and snacks.
- **Additional Activities:** Take the cable car for a shorter hike or enjoy a meal at Rifugio Scoiattoli or Rifugio Cinque Torri.

- **Safety:** Check weather forecasts before setting out, carry a map or GPS, and be cautious on rocky sections.

The hike to the Cinque Torri offers a unique blend of natural beauty and historical significance, making it an exciting and educational experience for hikers of all levels.

Walk 23: Up the Nuvolau

Highlights

- **Stunning Summit Views:** Panoramic vistas from the summit of Mount Nuvolau, including views of the Marmolada, Tofana, and Civetta.
- **Rifugio Experience:** Visit the historic Rifugio Nuvolau at the summit for refreshments and a unique mountain experience.
- **Varied Terrain:** A mix of rocky paths, alpine meadows, and rugged terrain.

Route Description

- **Starting Point:** Passo Giau parking area.
- **Distance:** Approximately 6 km (3.7 miles) round trip.
- **Duration:** 3 to 4 hours.
- **Route:** Start from the Passo Giau parking area and follow trail no. 443 towards Rifugio Nuvolau. The path ascends steadily, passing through meadows and

rocky sections. As you approach the summit, the trail becomes steeper and more rugged. Reach Rifugio Nuvolau at the summit, where you can rest and enjoy the breathtaking views. Descend via the same route back to the starting point.

Tips and Recommendations

- **Best Time to Visit:** Late spring to early autumn for optimal weather and trail conditions.
- **Gear:** Sturdy hiking boots, layered clothing, sun protection, water, and snacks.
- **Additional Activities:** Enjoy a meal or drink at Rifugio Nuvolau and take in the panoramic views. Capture photos of the surrounding peaks and valleys.
- **Safety:** Check weather forecasts before setting out, carry a map or GPS, and be prepared for sudden weather changes. Use caution on the steeper, rocky sections of the trail.

Walk 24: Skirting the Tofana di Rozes

Highlights

- **Imposing Peaks:** Majestic views of Tofana di Rozes, one of the most impressive mountains in the Dolomites.
- **Diverse Scenery:** Varied landscapes including alpine meadows, rocky paths, and dense forests.
- **Historical Interest:** Remnants of World War I tunnels and fortifications.

Route Description

- **Starting Point:** Rifugio Dibona parking area.
- **Distance:** Approximately 12 km (7.5 miles) round trip.
- **Duration:** 5 to 6 hours.
- **Route:** Begin at the Rifugio Dibona parking area and follow trail no. 404 towards Rifugio Giussani. The path ascends through meadows and rocky terrain, skirting the base of Tofana di Rozes. Continue to Rifugio Giussani for a break and enjoy the panoramic views. From there, follow trail no. 403 and loop back towards Rifugio Dibona, passing through varied landscapes and offering continuous views of the Tofana massif.

Tips and Recommendations

- **Best Time to Visit:** Late spring to early autumn for the best weather and trail conditions.
- **Gear:** Sturdy hiking boots, layered clothing, sun protection, water, and snacks.
- **Additional Activities:** Explore the World War I tunnels and fortifications along the route. Enjoy a meal or refreshments at Rifugio Giussani.
- **Safety:** Check weather forecasts before setting out, carry a map or GPS, and be prepared for sudden weather changes. Use caution on rocky sections and be aware of potential loose stones.

Skirting the Tofana di Rozes offers a challenging yet rewarding hike with diverse landscapes, historical interest, and some of the most stunning views in the Dolomites, making it a must-do for experienced hikers.

Walk 25: The Lagazuoi Tunnels

Highlights

- **Historical Tunnels:** Explore the extensive World War I tunnel system built into Mount Lagazuoi.
- **Panoramic Views:** Breathtaking vistas of the Dolomite peaks from the summit.
- **Unique Experience:** A combination of hiking and historical exploration.

Route Description

- **Starting Point:** Passo Falzarego parking area.
- **Distance:** Approximately 9 km (5.6 miles) round trip.
- **Duration:** 4 to 5 hours.
- **Route:** Begin at the Passo Falzarego parking area and take the Lagazuoi cable car (optional) to Rifugio Lagazuoi. From the rifugio, follow the marked trail down to the entrance of the Lagazuoi tunnels. Equip yourself with a helmet and headlamp (available for rent at the rifugio) and descend through the tunnels, exploring the historical sites along the way. Exit the

tunnels at the base and return to Passo Falzarego via trail no. 402.

Tips and Recommendations

- **Best Time to Visit:** Late spring to early autumn for optimal weather and trail conditions.
- **Gear:** Sturdy hiking boots, layered clothing, sun protection, water, and snacks. A helmet and headlamp are essential for tunnel exploration.
- **Additional Activities:** Visit the open-air museum at the top of Lagazuoi for more historical insights. Enjoy a meal or drink at Rifugio Lagazuoi.
- **Safety:** Check weather forecasts before setting out, carry a map or GPS, and be prepared for sudden weather changes. The tunnels can be slippery and dark, so proceed with caution and use appropriate gear.

The Lagazuoi Tunnels hike offers a unique combination of natural beauty and historical exploration, making it an unforgettable experience for those interested in both hiking and history.

Walk 26: The Kaiserjäger Route

Highlights

- **Historical Significance:** Follow the historic World War I military route used by the Austrian Kaiserjäger troops.
- **Dramatic Scenery:** Stunning views of the Dolomites, including the Lagazuoi and Tofana di Rozes.
- **Unique Experience:** Traverse tunnels, ladders, and exposed paths with historical remnants along the way.

Route Description

- **Starting Point:** Passo Falzarego parking area.
- **Distance:** Approximately 7 km (4.3 miles) round trip.
- **Duration:** 4 to 5 hours.
- **Route:** Start at the Passo Falzarego parking area and take the Lagazuoi cable car (optional) to Rifugio Lagazuoi. From there, follow the Kaiserjäger route (Via Ferrata) down the mountain. The path includes sections of tunnels, ladders, and exposed trails with fixed cables for safety. The route offers continuous breathtaking views and historical insights. Return to the starting point via trail no. 402.

Tips and Recommendations

- **Best Time to Visit:** Late spring to early autumn for optimal weather and trail conditions.
- **Gear:** Sturdy hiking boots, via ferrata kit (harness, helmet, and lanyards), layered clothing, sun protection, water, and snacks.
- **Additional Activities:** Visit the Lagazuoi open-air museum and enjoy a meal at Rifugio Lagazuoi.

- **Safety:** This route includes via ferrata sections, so it is essential to have the appropriate equipment and experience. Check weather forecasts before setting out, carry a map or GPS, and be prepared for sudden weather changes.

Walk 27: Round the Settsass

Highlights

- **Scenic Loop:** Complete circuit around the Settsass massif, offering varied landscapes and stunning views.
- **Diverse Terrain:** A mix of alpine meadows, rocky paths, and panoramic viewpoints.
- **Flora and Fauna:** Opportunities to spot local wildlife and enjoy the diverse plant life.

Route Description

- **Starting Point:** Passo Valparola parking area.
- **Distance:** Approximately 14 km (8.7 miles) round trip.
- **Duration:** 5 to 6 hours.
- **Route:** Begin at the Passo Valparola parking area and follow trail no. 23 towards the Settsass massif. The trail ascends gently through meadows and rocky terrain, offering beautiful views of the surrounding peaks. Continue around the base of Settsass, passing through diverse landscapes. The path loops back

towards Passo Valparola, providing a complete circuit with continuous scenic vistas.

Tips and Recommendations

- **Best Time to Visit:** Late spring to early autumn for optimal weather and trail conditions.
- **Gear:** Sturdy hiking boots, layered clothing, sun protection, water, and snacks.
- **Additional Activities:** Bring a camera for capturing the panoramic views and take breaks to enjoy the tranquil alpine environment.
- **Safety:** Check weather forecasts before setting out, carry a map or GPS, and be prepared for sudden weather changes. Be cautious on rocky sections and ensure you have enough provisions for a full day hike.

The hike around the Settsass offers a rewarding experience with diverse terrain, stunning views, and the opportunity to immerse yourself in the natural beauty of the Dolomites.

Walk 28: Santa Croce Sanctuary

Highlights

- **Spiritual Experience:** Visit the historic Santa Croce Sanctuary, a significant pilgrimage site.
- **Panoramic Views:** Stunning vistas of the surrounding Dolomite peaks and valleys.

- **Cultural Interest:** Explore the sanctuary and its rich history.

Route Description

- **Starting Point:** Badia (San Leonardo) parking area.
- **Distance:** Approximately 10 km (6.2 miles) round trip.
- **Duration:** 4 to 5 hours.
- **Route:** Begin at the Badia (San Leonardo) parking area and follow trail no. 7 towards the Santa Croce Sanctuary. The path ascends gradually through forests and meadows, offering beautiful views along the way. Reach the sanctuary and take time to explore the historic church and its surroundings. Return via the same route, enjoying the panoramic vistas on the descent.

Tips and Recommendations

- **Best Time to Visit:** Late spring to early autumn for optimal weather and trail conditions.
- **Gear:** Comfortable hiking shoes, layered clothing, sun protection, water, and snacks.
- **Additional Activities:** Spend time exploring the sanctuary and its history. Enjoy a meal or refreshments at the nearby Rifugio La Crusc.
- **Safety:** Check weather forecasts before setting out, carry a map or GPS, and be prepared for sudden weather changes. Ensure you have enough provisions for a full day hike.

Walk 29: Sass de Putia

Highlights

- **Iconic Mountain:** Stunning views of Sass de Putia, a prominent peak in the Dolomites.
- **360-Degree Panoramas:** Breathtaking vistas from the summit and along the trail.
- **Diverse Terrain:** A mix of alpine meadows, rocky paths, and lush forests.

Route Description

- **Starting Point:** Passo delle Erbe parking area.
- **Distance:** Approximately 12 km (7.5 miles) round trip.
- **Duration:** 5 to 6 hours.
- **Route:** Begin at the Passo delle Erbe parking area and follow trail no. 8 towards Forcella de Putia. The trail ascends gradually through meadows and forests, leading to the Forcella de Putia pass. From here, follow the path up to the summit of Sass de Putia for panoramic views. Descend via the same route to the pass, then take trail no. 4 to complete the loop around the mountain, returning to the starting point.

Tips and Recommendations

- **Best Time to Visit:** Late spring to early autumn for optimal weather and trail conditions.
- **Gear:** Sturdy hiking boots, layered clothing, sun protection, water, and snacks.
- **Additional Activities:** Enjoy a picnic at the summit or along the trail, and take plenty of photos of the stunning scenery.
- **Safety:** Check weather forecasts before setting out, carry a map or GPS, and be prepared for sudden weather changes. Use caution on the rocky sections, especially near the summit.

The hike around Sass de Putia offers a rewarding experience with diverse landscapes and panoramic views, making it a must-do for hikers exploring the Dolomites.

Walk 30: Sentiero delle Odle

Highlights

- **Stunning Scenery:** Breathtaking views of the Odle (Geisler) peaks.
- **Diverse Landscapes:** Mix of alpine meadows, dense forests, and rugged mountain terrain.
- **Photographic Opportunities:** Numerous spots for capturing the majestic beauty of the Dolomites.

Route Description

- **Starting Point:** Zannes parking area.
- **Distance:** Approximately 10 km (6.2 miles) round trip.
- **Duration:** 4 to 5 hours.
- **Route:** Begin at the Zannes parking area and follow trail no. 6 to Rifugio delle Odle. Continue on the Sentiero delle Odle (trail no. 35), which traverses beneath the impressive Odle peaks. The trail loops back towards Rifugio delle Odle and then returns to the Zannes parking area via trail no. 6.

Tips and Recommendations

- **Best Time to Visit:** Late spring to early autumn for the best weather and trail conditions.
- **Gear:** Sturdy hiking boots, layered clothing, sun protection, water, and snacks.
- **Additional Activities:** Stop at Rifugio delle Odle for refreshments and enjoy the panoramic views from the terrace. Capture photos of the scenic landscape.
- **Safety:** Check weather forecasts before setting out, carry a map or GPS, and be prepared for sudden weather changes. Use caution on rocky or slippery sections of the trail.

The Sentiero delle Odle offers a rewarding hike with stunning views, diverse terrain, and excellent photographic opportunities, making it a must-do for nature lovers exploring the Dolomites.

Walk 31: The Rasciesa Ridge

Highlights

- **Panoramic Views:** Stunning vistas of the Dolomite peaks and valleys from the Rasciesa Ridge.
- **Peaceful Trails:** Less crowded paths offering a serene hiking experience.
- **Diverse Scenery:** Mix of alpine meadows, rocky ridges, and forested areas.

Route Description

- **Starting Point:** Ortisei (St. Ulrich) funicular station.
- **Distance:** Approximately 11 km (6.8 miles) round trip.
- **Duration:** 4 to 5 hours.
- **Route:** Start at the Ortisei funicular station and take the funicular up to the Rasciesa Ridge. From the top station, follow trail no. 35 along the ridge, enjoying panoramic views of the surrounding peaks. Continue to the Rasciesa Chapel and then loop back along trail no. 10, which descends through meadows and forests. Return to the starting point via the same funicular.

Tips and Recommendations

- **Best Time to Visit:** Late spring to early autumn for optimal weather and trail conditions.
- **Gear:** Comfortable hiking boots, layered clothing, sun protection, water, and snacks.

- **Additional Activities:** Enjoy a picnic with a view at the Rasciesa Chapel and take plenty of photos of the scenic vistas.
- **Safety:** Check weather forecasts before setting out, carry a map or GPS, and be prepared for sudden weather changes. The trail is generally easy to moderate, but use caution on rocky sections.

Walk 32: Across the Puez-Odle Altopiano

Highlights

- **Stunning Plateau Views:** Expansive vistas of the Puez-Odle Altopiano and surrounding Dolomite peaks.
- **Diverse Terrain:** A mix of high-altitude meadows, rocky paths, and dramatic cliffs.
- **Wildlife and Flora:** Opportunities to spot local wildlife and enjoy diverse alpine flora.

Route Description

- **Starting Point:** Colfosco parking area.
- **Distance:** Approximately 16 km (10 miles) round trip.
- **Duration:** 6 to 7 hours.

- **Route:** Begin at the Colfosco parking area and follow trail no. 4 towards Rifugio Puez. The trail ascends steadily through Val de Misdé, reaching the Puez-Odle Altopiano. Continue across the plateau, enjoying panoramic views and diverse landscapes. From Rifugio Puez, follow trail no. 2 to descend into the Vallunga valley and return to the starting point.

Tips and Recommendations

- **Best Time to Visit:** Late spring to early autumn for optimal weather and trail conditions.
- **Gear:** Sturdy hiking boots, layered clothing, sun protection, water, and snacks.
- **Additional Activities:** Stop at Rifugio Puez for a meal or refreshments and take time to enjoy the panoramic views from the plateau.
- **Safety:** Check weather forecasts before setting out, carry a map or GPS, and be prepared for sudden weather changes. Ensure you have enough provisions for a full day hike, as the trail covers remote areas.

Walk 33: The Bullaccia Tour

Highlights

- **Scenic Views:** Panoramic vistas of the Dolomites, including the Sella Group and Sassolungo.

- **Alpine Meadows:** Beautiful meadows filled with wildflowers in the summer.
- **Cultural Interest:** Traditional mountain huts and local alpine culture.

Route Description

- **Starting Point:** Compatsch parking area, Alpe di Siusi.
- **Distance:** Approximately 10 km (6.2 miles) round trip.
- **Duration:** 4 to 5 hours.
- **Route:** Begin at the Compatsch parking area and follow trail no. 14 towards Bullaccia (Puflatsch). The path ascends gradually through alpine meadows and offers stunning views of the surrounding peaks. Continue to the Bullaccia viewpoint, then loop back via trail no. 14B, passing by traditional mountain huts. The route provides continuous scenic vistas and a pleasant hiking experience.

Tips and Recommendations

- **Best Time to Visit:** Late spring to early autumn for the best weather and trail conditions.
- **Gear:** Comfortable hiking shoes, layered clothing, sun protection, water, and snacks.
- **Additional Activities:** Enjoy a meal or refreshments at one of the mountain huts and take time to capture photos of the panoramic views.

- **Safety:** Check weather forecasts before setting out, carry a map or GPS, and be prepared for sudden weather changes. The trail is generally easy to moderate but use caution on steeper sections.

Walk 34: Alpe di Siusi Circuit and Rifugio Bolzano

Highlights

- **Expansive Meadows:** Hike through the largest high-altitude alpine meadow in Europe.
- **Rifugio Experience:** Visit Rifugio Bolzano for local cuisine and stunning views.
- **Panoramic Vistas:** Spectacular views of the Dolomite peaks, including the Sassolungo and Sciliar mountains.

Route Description

- **Starting Point:** Compatsch parking area, Alpe di Siusi.
- **Distance:** Approximately 14 km (8.7 miles) round trip.
- **Duration:** 5 to 6 hours.
- **Route:** Start at the Compatsch parking area and follow trail no. 5 towards Rifugio Bolzano. The path ascends gradually through the picturesque meadows of Alpe di Siusi, offering beautiful views of the

surrounding peaks. Continue on trail no. 1 to reach Rifugio Bolzano, where you can take a break and enjoy the panoramic views. Loop back to the starting point via trail no. 7A, passing through diverse landscapes of meadows and forests.

Tips and Recommendations

- **Best Time to Visit:** Late spring to early autumn for the best weather and trail conditions.
- **Gear:** Sturdy hiking boots, layered clothing, sun protection, water, and snacks.
- **Additional Activities:** Enjoy a meal or refreshments at Rifugio Bolzano and take in the stunning views from the terrace. Capture photos of the expansive meadows and towering peaks.
- **Safety:** Check weather forecasts before setting out, carry a map or GPS, and be prepared for sudden weather changes. Ensure you have enough provisions for a full day hike.

Walk 35: Castel Presule

Highlights

- **Historical Castle:** Explore the beautiful Castel Presule, a well-preserved medieval castle.
- **Scenic Countryside:** Enjoy the picturesque landscapes of the surrounding countryside.

- **Cultural Experience:** Learn about the history and architecture of the region.

Route Description

- **Starting Point:** Fiè allo Sciliar (Völs am Schlern) parking area.
- **Distance:** Approximately 8 km (5 miles) round trip.
- **Duration:** 3 to 4 hours.
- **Route:** Begin at the Fiè allo Sciliar parking area and follow trail no. 3 towards Castel Presule. The path meanders through charming villages, vineyards, and forests, gradually ascending to the castle. Take time to explore the castle grounds and learn about its history. After your visit, return to the starting point via the same route, enjoying the scenic views along the way.

Tips and Recommendations

- **Best Time to Visit:** Late spring to early autumn for optimal weather and trail conditions.
- **Gear:** Comfortable walking shoes, layered clothing, sun protection, water, and snacks.
- **Additional Activities:** Plan a guided tour of Castel Presule to fully appreciate its history and architecture. Enjoy a picnic in the castle's scenic surroundings.
- **Safety:** Check weather forecasts before setting out, carry a map or GPS, and be prepared for sudden weather changes.

Walk 36: Val Ciamin

Highlights

- **Serene Valley:** Enjoy the tranquil beauty of Val Ciamin, a lesser-known gem in the Dolomites.
- **Diverse Flora and Fauna:** Spot various alpine plants and local wildlife along the trail.
- **Scenic Views:** Beautiful landscapes featuring forests, meadows, and mountain streams.

Route Description

- **Starting Point:** Tiers (Tires) parking area.
- **Distance:** Approximately 10 km (6.2 miles) round trip.
- **Duration:** 4 to 5 hours.
- **Route:** Begin at the Tiers parking area and follow trail no. 3 into Val Ciamin. The path ascends gradually through dense forests and opens up to scenic meadows and streams. Continue along the well-marked trail, enjoying the peaceful surroundings and picturesque views. Loop back to the starting point via trail no. 4, which offers a slightly different perspective of the valley.

Tips and Recommendations

- **Best Time to Visit:** Late spring to early autumn for optimal weather and trail conditions.
- **Gear:** Comfortable hiking shoes, layered clothing, sun protection, water, and snacks.
- **Additional Activities:** Bring binoculars for birdwatching and a camera to capture the serene landscapes. Enjoy a picnic in one of the meadows.
- **Safety:** Check weather forecasts before setting out, carry a map or GPS, and be prepared for sudden weather changes. Ensure you have enough provisions for a full day hike.

Walk 37: The Inner Catinaccio

Highlights

- **Dramatic Rock Formations:** Explore the stunning peaks and cliffs of the Catinaccio (Rosengarten) range.
- **Alpine Meadows:** Beautiful meadows with diverse flora and panoramic views.
- **Rifugio Experience:** Visit mountain huts for refreshments and rest.

Route Description

- **Starting Point:** Ciampedie cable car station, Vigo di Fassa.

- **Distance:** Approximately 12 km (7.5 miles) round trip.
- **Duration:** 5 to 6 hours.
- **Route:** Start at the Ciampedie cable car station and take the cable car up to the Ciampedie plateau. From there, follow trail no. 541 towards Rifugio Vajolet. Continue to Rifugio Preuss, enjoying the dramatic views of the Catinaccio range. Follow trail no. 542 up to Passo Principe, then descend towards Rifugio Gardeccia. Return to the Ciampedie cable car station via trail no. 546, completing the loop.

Tips and Recommendations

- **Best Time to Visit:** Late spring to early autumn for optimal weather and trail conditions.
- **Gear:** Sturdy hiking boots, layered clothing, sun protection, water, and snacks.
- **Additional Activities:** Enjoy a meal or refreshments at the mountain huts and take time to explore the unique rock formations. Capture photos of the panoramic views.
- **Safety:** Check weather forecasts before setting out, carry a map or GPS, and be prepared for sudden weather changes. Use caution on rocky sections and ensure you have enough provisions for a full day hike.

Walk 38: Sentiero del Masaré

Highlights

- **Spectacular Views:** Breathtaking vistas of the Dolomites and Lake Carezza.
- **Challenging Terrain:** A mix of rocky paths, alpine meadows, and dramatic cliffs.
- **Unique Experience:** Traverse exposed sections with fixed cables for safety.

Route Description

- **Starting Point:** Lake Carezza parking area.
- **Distance:** Approximately 8 km (5 miles) round trip.
- **Duration:** 4 to 5 hours.
- **Route:** Begin at the Lake Carezza parking area and follow trail no. 549 towards the Latemar massif. The path ascends through forests and rocky sections, reaching the start of the Sentiero del Masaré. Traverse the exposed sections with fixed cables, enjoying stunning views of the Dolomites. Continue on trail no. 18 towards Rifugio Roda di Vael, where you can take a break. Descend back to the starting point via trail no. 517, passing through alpine meadows and forests.

Tips and Recommendations

- **Best Time to Visit:** Late spring to early autumn for optimal weather and trail conditions.
- **Gear:** Sturdy hiking boots, via ferrata kit (harness, helmet, and lanyards), layered clothing, sun protection, water, and snacks.

- **Additional Activities:** Enjoy a meal or refreshments at Rifugio Roda di Vael and take in the panoramic views from the terrace. Capture photos of the dramatic scenery.
- **Safety:** This route includes via ferrata sections, so it is essential to have the appropriate equipment and experience. Check weather forecasts before setting out, carry a map or GPS, and be prepared for sudden weather changes. Use caution on exposed sections and ensure you have enough provisions for a full day hike.

The Sentiero del Masaré offers a thrilling and rewarding hike with spectacular views and challenging terrain, making it an unforgettable experience for experienced hikers and via ferrata enthusiasts in the Dolomites.

Walk 39: The Latemar Labyrinth and Lago di Carezza

Highlights

- **Natural Labyrinth:** Explore the unique rock formations of the Latemar Labyrinth.
- **Scenic Lake:** Beautiful views of Lago di Carezza, known for its crystal-clear waters.
- **Diverse Terrain:** A mix of forest trails, rocky paths, and alpine meadows.

Route Description

- **Starting Point:** Lake Carezza parking area.
- **Distance:** Approximately 8 km (5 miles) round trip.
- **Duration:** 3 to 4 hours.
- **Route:** Begin at the Lake Carezza parking area and follow trail no. 18 towards the Latemar Labyrinth. Navigate through the intricate rock formations, then continue towards Lago di Carezza. Enjoy the scenic views around the lake before returning to the starting point via trail no. 6.

Tips and Recommendations

- **Best Time to Visit:** Late spring to early autumn for optimal weather and trail conditions.
- **Gear:** Comfortable hiking shoes, layered clothing, sun protection, water, and snacks.

- **Additional Activities:** Bring a camera to capture the stunning views and unique rock formations. Enjoy a picnic by the lake.
- **Safety:** Check weather forecasts before setting out, carry a map or GPS, and be prepared for sudden weather changes.

Walk 40:

Circumnavigating Sassopiatto-Sassolungo

Highlights

- **Impressive Peaks:** Circumnavigate the dramatic Sassopiatto and Sassolungo mountains.
- **Panoramic Views:** Stunning vistas of the surrounding Dolomite peaks and valleys.
- **Alpine Meadows:** Beautiful meadows with diverse flora and fauna.

Route Description

- **Starting Point:** Passo Sella parking area.
- **Distance:** Approximately 17 km (10.6 miles) round trip.
- **Duration:** 6 to 7 hours.
- **Route:** Begin at the Passo Sella parking area and follow trail no. 526 around the Sassopiatto and Sassolungo massif. The trail passes through alpine

meadows and rocky terrain, offering continuous panoramic views. Complete the loop by returning to the starting point via trail no. 527.

Tips and Recommendations

- **Best Time to Visit:** Late spring to early autumn for optimal weather and trail conditions.
- **Gear:** Sturdy hiking boots, layered clothing, sun protection, water, and snacks.
- **Additional Activities:** Stop at one of the mountain huts along the route for refreshments. Capture photos of the impressive peaks and landscapes.
- **Safety:** Check weather forecasts before setting out, carry a map or GPS, and be prepared for sudden weather changes.

Walk 41: The Sella and Piz Boë

Highlights

- **High-Altitude Scenery:** Experience the stunning views from the Sella massif and the summit of Piz Boë.
- **Challenging Terrain:** A mix of rocky paths, high-altitude meadows, and exposed sections.
- **Panoramic Vistas:** Breathtaking views of the Dolomites from the summit.

Route Description

- **Starting Point:** Passo Pordoi parking area.
- **Distance:** Approximately 12 km (7.5 miles) round trip.
- **Duration:** 5 to 6 hours.
- **Route:** Begin at the Passo Pordoi parking area and take the cable car to Sass Pordoi. From there, follow trail no. 627 towards Piz Boë. The path ascends through rocky terrain, reaching the summit for panoramic views. Descend via the same route or take trail no. 638 to Rifugio Boè and return to the starting point.

Tips and Recommendations

- **Best Time to Visit:** Late spring to early autumn for optimal weather and trail conditions.
- **Gear:** Sturdy hiking boots, layered clothing, sun protection, water, and snacks.
- **Additional Activities:** Enjoy a meal or refreshments at Rifugio Boè. Capture photos from the summit.
- **Safety:** This hike includes exposed sections and high-altitude terrain. Check weather forecasts before setting out, carry a map or GPS, and use caution on rocky sections.

Walk 42: Viel del Pan

Highlights

- **Historic Trail:** Follow the ancient Viel del Pan route, used by traders and pilgrims.
- **Scenic Views:** Stunning vistas of the Marmolada glacier and surrounding peaks.
- **Alpine Experience:** A mix of meadows, rocky paths, and historical landmarks.

Route Description

- **Starting Point:** Passo Pordoi parking area.
- **Distance:** Approximately 8 km (5 miles) round trip.
- **Duration:** 3 to 4 hours.
- **Route:** Begin at the Passo Pordoi parking area and follow trail no. 601 along the Viel del Pan. The path offers stunning views of the Marmolada glacier and the surrounding Dolomite peaks. Continue to Rifugio Viel del Pan for a break, then return via the same route.

Tips and Recommendations

- **Best Time to Visit:** Late spring to early autumn for optimal weather and trail conditions.
- **Gear:** Comfortable hiking shoes, layered clothing, sun protection, water, and snacks.

- **Additional Activities:** Enjoy a meal or refreshments at Rifugio Viel del Pan. Capture photos of the Marmolada glacier and surrounding scenery.
- **Safety:** Check weather forecasts before setting out, carry a map or GPS, and be prepared for sudden weather changes.

Walk 43: The Sas de Adam Crest

Highlights

- **Dramatic Crest:** Traverse the stunning Sas de Adam crest with panoramic views.
- **Challenging Terrain:** A mix of rocky paths, alpine meadows, and exposed sections.
- **Scenic Vistas:** Breathtaking views of the surrounding Dolomite peaks and valleys.

Route Description

- **Starting Point:** Passo delle Erbe parking area.
- **Distance:** Approximately 10 km (6.2 miles) round trip.
- **Duration:** 4 to 5 hours.
- **Route:** Begin at the Passo delle Erbe parking area and follow trail no. 8 towards the Sas de Adam crest. The path ascends through meadows and rocky sections, reaching the crest for panoramic views. Continue

along the crest and descend back to the starting point via trail no. 4.

Tips and Recommendations

- **Best Time to Visit:** Late spring to early autumn for optimal weather and trail conditions.
- **Gear:** Sturdy hiking boots, layered clothing, sun protection, water, and snacks.
- **Additional Activities:** Bring a camera to capture the stunning views from the crest. Enjoy a picnic with a view.
- **Safety:** This route includes exposed sections and rocky terrain. Check weather forecasts before setting out, carry a map or GPS, and use caution on rocky sections.

Walk 44: The Marmolada and Punta Serauta

Highlights

- **Highest Peak:** Experience the stunning views from the highest peak in the Dolomites, Marmolada.
- **Glacial Scenery:** Traverse the Marmolada glacier and enjoy breathtaking ice views.
- **Historical Interest:** Visit World War I sites and the open-air museum at Punta Serauta.

Route Description

- **Starting Point:** Malga Ciapela parking area.
- **Distance:** Approximately 9 km (5.6 miles) round trip.
- **Duration:** 5 to 6 hours.
- **Route:** Begin at the Malga Ciapela parking area and take the cable car to Punta Rocca. From there, follow the marked trail to Punta Serauta, traversing the glacier. Explore the World War I open-air museum and enjoy panoramic views. Return via the same route to the cable car station.

Tips and Recommendations

- **Best Time to Visit:** Late spring to early autumn for optimal weather and trail conditions.
- **Gear:** Sturdy hiking boots, layered clothing, sun protection, water, snacks, and glacier equipment if necessary.
- **Additional Activities:** Visit the open-air museum and take photos of the glacial scenery. Enjoy a meal at the mountain hut.
- **Safety:** This hike involves high-altitude terrain and glacier travel. Check weather forecasts before setting out, carry a map or GPS, and use caution on icy sections.

Walk 45: Rifugio Falier in Valle Ombretta

Highlights

- **Stunning Valley:** Explore the beautiful Valle Ombretta with dramatic mountain views.
- **Rifugio Experience:** Visit Rifugio Falier for local cuisine and stunning vistas.
- **Diverse Terrain:** A mix of meadows, forests, and rocky paths.

Route Description

- **Starting Point:** Malga Ciapela parking area.
- **Distance:** Approximately 10 km (6.2 miles) round trip.
- **Duration:** 4 to 5 hours.
- **Route:** Begin at the Malga Ciapela parking area and follow trail no. 610 towards Rifugio Falier. The path ascends gradually through meadows and forests, offering beautiful views of the surrounding peaks. Continue to Rifugio Falier for a break and enjoy the panoramic views. Return via the same route to the starting point.

Tips and Recommendations

- **Best Time to Visit:** Late spring to early autumn for optimal weather and trail conditions.
- **Gear:** Comfortable hiking shoes, layered clothing, sun protection, water, and snacks.
- **Additional Activities:** Enjoy a meal or refreshments at Rifugio Falier. Capture photos of the scenic valley and dramatic peaks.

- **Safety:** Check weather forecasts before setting out, carry a map or GPS, and be prepared for sudden weather changes.

One-Week Itinerary

Day 1: Arrival and Exploration of Bolzano

Morning:

- Arrival in Bolzano: Fly into Venice Marco Polo Airport or Verona Villafranca Airport and take a train or shuttle to Bolzano.

- Check-In: Arrive at your hotel in Bolzano, such as Hotel Greif or Parkhotel Laurin.

Afternoon:

- Explore Bolzano: Wander through the charming streets of Bolzano, visiting the South Tyrol Museum of Archaeology to see Ötzi the Iceman.

- Lunch: Enjoy a traditional South Tyrolean meal at a local restaurant, such as Batzenhäusl.

Evening:

- Cable Car to Renon: Take the Renon cable car for stunning views of the Dolomites and a peaceful walk on the Renon plateau.

- Dinner: Return to Bolzano for dinner at a local pizzeria or fine dining restaurant.

Day 2: Alpe di Siusi and Castel Presule

Morning;

- Drive to Alpe di Siusi: Head to Compatsch parking area in Alpe di Siusi, the largest high-altitude alpine meadow in Europe.

- Hike the Alpe di Siusi Circuit: Follow trail no. 5 towards Rifugio Bolzano, enjoying expansive meadows and panoramic views.

Afternoon:

- Lunch at Rifugio Bolzano: Savor local cuisine while taking in the stunning scenery.

- Castel Presule: Drive to Castel Presule and explore the well-preserved medieval castle.

Evening:

- Return to Bolzano: Enjoy a relaxing evening, strolling through the town or visiting a local café.

Day 3: Val Gardena and the Sella Pass

Morning:

- Drive to Val Gardena: Head to the picturesque valley of Val Gardena, known for its charming villages and stunning views.

- Hike the Rasciesa Ridge: Take the funicular from Ortisei and hike along the Rasciesa Ridge, enjoying panoramic vistas.

Afternoon:

- Lunch in Ortisei: Have a meal at a local restaurant, such as Tubladel, featuring traditional Ladin cuisine.

- Sella Pass: Drive to the Sella Pass and enjoy short walks or a scenic drive through this iconic mountain pass.

Evening:

- Check-In at a Rifugio: Stay overnight at Rifugio Passo Sella or Rifugio Boé for an authentic mountain experience.

- Dinner at the Rifugio: Enjoy a hearty meal at the rifugio, savoring the mountain atmosphere.

Day 4: Tre Cime di Lavaredo and Lake Misurina

Morning:

- Drive to Tre Cime di Lavaredo: Head to Rifugio Auronzo parking area to start your hike.

- Hike the Tre Cime di Lavaredo Loop: Follow the well-marked trail around the iconic Tre Cime peaks, enjoying breathtaking views.

Afternoon:

- Lunch at Rifugio Locatelli: Take a break at Rifugio Locatelli for a meal with stunning mountain views.

- Lake Misurina: Drive to Lake Misurina and enjoy a leisurely walk around the lake.

Evening:

- Check-In at a Lake Misurina Hotel: Stay overnight at a lakeside hotel, such as Grand Hotel Misurina.

- Dinner: Dine at the hotel restaurant, enjoying views of the lake and surrounding peaks.

Day 5: Cortina d'Ampezzo and the Lagazuoi Tunnels

Morning:

- Drive to Cortina d'Ampezzo: Head to the chic town of Cortina, known for its upscale shops and stunning mountain scenery.

- Explore Cortina: Wander through the town, visiting local shops and enjoying the alpine atmosphere.

Afternoon:

- Lagazuoi Tunnels: Take the cable car from Passo Falzarego to Rifugio Lagazuoi. Explore the World War I tunnels and the open-air museum.

- Lunch at Rifugio Lagazuoi: Have a meal at the rifugio while enjoying panoramic views of the Dolomites.

Evening:

-Return to Cortina: Spend the evening in Cortina, dining at a local restaurant such as Ristorante Tivoli.

Day 6: Lago di Braies and Rifugio Biella Loop

Morning:

- Drive to Lago di Braies: Head to the stunning Lago di Braies, one of the most picturesque lakes in the Dolomites.

- Walk Around the Lake: Enjoy a leisurely walk around the lake, taking in the crystal-clear waters and surrounding peaks.

Afternoon:

- Drive to Malga Ra Stua: Start the hike to Rifugio Biella, following the trail through lush meadows and forests.

- Lunch at Rifugio Biella: Savor a meal at the rifugio with stunning mountain views.

Evening:

- Return to Bolzano:** Head back to Bolzano for your final night. Enjoy a relaxing evening and dinner at a local restaurant.

Day 7: Departure

Morning:

- Last-Minute Shopping: Spend your final morning shopping for souvenirs or visiting any missed attractions in Bolzano.

- Check-Out: Check out of your hotel and head to the airport for your departure.

Afternoon:

- Travel to Airport: Take a train or shuttle back to Venice Marco Polo Airport or Verona Villafranca Airport for your flight home.

Evening:

Flight Home: Depart from the Dolomites with unforgettable memories and a newfound appreciation for this stunning region.

By following this detailed itinerary, you'll experience the best of the Dolomites, from stunning hikes and picturesque lakes to charming towns and historical sites. You can adjust it to suit you.

Practical Information

When planning a trip to the Dolomites, having practical information at your fingertips can make your visit more enjoyable and stress-free. Here's a comprehensive guide to help you prepare for your adventure.

Getting There

By Air:

- **Venice Marco Polo Airport (VCE):** Approximately 150-200 km from the Dolomites.
- **Verona Villafranca Airport (VRN):** Approximately 150-200 km from the Dolomites.
- **Innsbruck Airport (INN):** Approximately 100-150 km from the Dolomites.
- **Milan Bergamo Airport (BGY):** Approximately 200-300 km from the Dolomites.
- **Treviso Airport (TSF):** Approximately 150 km from the Dolomites.

By Train:

- Trains connect major cities like Venice, Verona, and Milan to key transit hubs in the Dolomites, such as Bolzano, Trento, and Belluno. From these hubs, you can transfer to regional trains or buses to reach your destination.

By Bus:

- Regional buses operated by companies like SAD and Dolomitibus connect towns and villages within the Dolomites. FlixBus also offers routes from major cities to the Dolomites.

By Car:

- Renting a car provides flexibility for exploring the region. Major car rental services are available at airports and in larger towns. Ensure you are familiar with local driving regulations and have appropriate insurance coverage.

Accommodation

The Dolomites offer a range of accommodation options to suit all preferences and budgets:

- **Luxury Hotels and Resorts:** For a luxurious stay with top-notch amenities.
- **Mountain Huts (Rifugios):** For an authentic alpine experience with stunning views.
- **Bed and Breakfasts:** Cozy and comfortable with a personal touch.
- **Hostels:** Budget-friendly options for solo travelers and groups.
- **Camping:** Campsites are available for those who prefer the outdoors.

Best Time to Visit

- **Spring (April to June):** Ideal for wildflower viewing, moderate temperatures, and fewer crowds.
- **Summer (July to August):** Perfect for hiking, climbing, and outdoor activities, but expect more tourists.
- **Autumn (September to November):** Beautiful fall colors, cooler weather, and less crowded trails.
- **Winter (December to March):** Best for skiing, snowboarding, and winter sports.

What to Pack

- **Clothing:** Layered clothing for changing weather conditions, waterproof jacket, sturdy hiking boots, hat, and gloves.
- **Gear:** Hiking poles, a reliable backpack, a map or GPS device, and a first-aid kit.
- **Other Essentials:** Sunscreen, sunglasses, a reusable water bottle, snacks, and a camera.
- **Winter Gear:** Thermal layers, ski jacket, pants, and other necessary ski equipment if visiting in winter.

Safety Tips

- **Trail Awareness:** Stick to marked trails and be aware of your surroundings.
- **Weather:** Check the weather forecast before heading out and be prepared for sudden changes.
- **Altitude:** Take it slow at higher altitudes and stay hydrated to avoid altitude sickness.

- **Local Rules:** Respect local regulations and guidelines, including wildlife and environmental conservation.

Local Etiquette and Customs

- **Language:** While many locals speak English, learning basic Italian or German phrases can be helpful.
- **Dining:** It is customary to say "Buon appetito" before starting a meal. Tipping is appreciated but not obligatory.
- **Respect for Nature:** Follow Leave No Trace principles to protect the natural environment.
- **Public Transport:** Be punctual and validate your tickets before boarding.

Emergency Contacts

- **Mountain Rescue:** Dial 112 for emergency services.
- **Tourist Information Centers:** Located in most towns and villages, providing maps, guides, and local information.
- **Pharmacies:** Available in towns for medical supplies and advice.

Resources

- **Maps and Guidebooks:** Available at tourist information centers, bookstores, and online.
- **Apps:** Download hiking and navigation apps like Komoot or AllTrails for detailed route information.

- **Local Guides:** Consider hiring a local guide for in-depth knowledge and safe exploration of remote areas.

By following this practical information, you'll be well-prepared for an unforgettable adventure in the Dolomites, ensuring a safe, enjoyable, and enriching experience.

Transportation Tips for Visiting the Dolomites

Navigating the Dolomites can be a seamless experience with the right transportation tips. Here's a comprehensive guide to help you get around efficiently and enjoy your trip.

Airports and Transfers

Major Airports:

- **Venice Marco Polo Airport (VCE):** Ideal for accessing the southern and central Dolomites.
- **Verona Villafranca Airport (VRN):** Convenient for the western Dolomites.
- **Innsbruck Airport (INN):** Best for the northern Dolomites.
- **Milan Bergamo Airport (BGY):** Good for the western Dolomites.
- **Treviso Airport (TSF):** Another option for the central Dolomites.

Airport Transfers:

- **Shuttle Services:** Many airports offer shuttle services to major towns in the Dolomites. Check for services like Terravision or FlixBus.
- **Private Transfers:** Book private transfers for direct travel to your accommodation. Companies like Suntransfers provide reliable options.

Car Rentals

- **Rental Locations:** Available at major airports and cities like Venice, Verona, and Bolzano.
- **Driving Tips:**
    - **Navigation:** Use GPS or a reliable navigation app.
    - **Parking:** Check parking regulations and availability, especially in popular areas.
    - **Road Conditions:** Be prepared for winding mountain roads and possible snow in winter. Winter tires or chains may be required.

Public Transportation

Trains:

- **Main Stations:** Bolzano, Trento, Belluno, and Dobbiaco are key transit hubs.
- **Connections:** Trenitalia and Italo offer connections from major cities. Regional trains link to smaller towns.
- **Tickets:** Purchase tickets in advance online or at the station. Validate tickets before boarding.

Buses:

- **Regional Buses:** Companies like SAD, Dolomitibus, and FlixBus operate in the region.
- **Schedules:** Check timetables in advance, as service frequency can vary, especially off-season.
- **Tickets:** Buy tickets at bus stations, on the bus, or online. Validate tickets before boarding.

Cable Cars and Funiculars

- **Popular Routes:** Use cable cars and funiculars for easy access to high-altitude trails and scenic viewpoints. Notable routes include:
  - **Sass Pordoi Cable Car:** From Passo Pordoi to Sass Pordoi.
  - **Rasciesa Funicular:** From Ortisei to the Rasciesa Ridge.
  - **Ciampedie Cable Car:** From Vigo di Fassa to Ciampedie.
- **Operating Times:** Check seasonal operating times and weather conditions.

Biking

- **Rentals:** Available in many towns and villages. Electric bikes (e-bikes) are also an option for easier rides.
- **Paths:** The Dolomites offer dedicated cycling paths and scenic routes like the Sella Ronda Bike Day circuit.
- **Safety:** Wear a helmet and follow local traffic rules. Be cautious on mountain roads.

Hiking and Walking

- **Trailheads:** Many hikes start from towns accessible by public transport or car. Plan your route to the trailhead in advance.

- **Maps and Apps:** Use detailed maps or hiking apps like Komoot and AllTrails for navigation.

Practical Tips

- **Weather Awareness:** Mountain weather can change rapidly. Always check forecasts and be prepared for sudden changes.
- **Local Transport Passes:** Consider purchasing local transport passes for unlimited travel on buses and trains in specific areas.
- **Tourist Information Centers:** Visit these centers for up-to-date transport schedules, maps, and local advice.

Emergency Numbers

- **General Emergency:** Dial 112 for assistance.
- **Mountain Rescue:** Specific services may be available in different areas.

Emergency Contacts and Services

Having quick access to emergency contacts and services can ensure your safety and provide peace of mind while exploring the Dolomites. Here's a comprehensive list of essential contacts and services to keep handy.

Emergency Contacts

General Emergency Number:

- **112:** The European emergency number for police, fire, and medical services.

Mountain Rescue:

- **118:** For mountain rescue services, including medical emergencies and accidents in remote areas.

Local Police (Carabinieri):

- **112:** For reporting crimes or incidents requiring police intervention.

Fire Department:

- **115:** For fire-related emergencies.

Medical Services:

- **118:** For medical emergencies requiring an ambulance or urgent medical assistance.

Forest Rangers (Corpo Forestale):

- **1515:** For reporting forest fires or wildlife emergencies.

Hospitals and Medical Facilities

Major Hospitals:

- **Ospedale di Bolzano (Bolzano Hospital):**
  - **Address:** Via Lorenz Böhler, 5, 39100 Bolzano BZ, Italy
  - **Phone:** +39 0471 908111
- **Ospedale di Trento (Santa Chiara Hospital):**
  - **Address:** Largo Medaglie d'Oro, 9, 38122 Trento TN, Italy
  - **Phone:** +39 0461 903111
- **Ospedale di Belluno (San Martino Hospital):**

- **Address:** Viale Europa, 22, 32100 Belluno BL, Italy
- **Phone:** +39 0437 516111

Pharmacies:

- Pharmacies (Farmacie) are available in towns and villages, providing medication and health advice. Look for the green cross symbol indicating a pharmacy.

Mountain Rescue Services

- **Corpo Nazionale Soccorso Alpino e Speleologico (CNSAS):** The national alpine and cave rescue service providing assistance in mountainous and remote areas.
  - **Website:** CNSAS

Tourist Information Centers

Tourist information centers can provide local advice, maps, and assistance:

- **Bolzano Tourist Information:**
  - **Address:** Piazza Walther, 8, 39100 Bolzano BZ, Italy
  - **Phone:** +39 0471 307000
- **Cortina d'Ampezzo Tourist Information:**
  - **Address:** Corso Italia, 81, 32043 Cortina d'Ampezzo BL, Italy
  - **Phone:** +39 0436 869086

- **Trento Tourist Information:**
  - **Address:** Piazza Dante, 24, 38122 Trento TN, Italy
  - **Phone:** +39 0461 216000

Weather and Trail Conditions

- **Dolomiti Meteo:** Check weather forecasts specific to the Dolomites.
  - **Website:** Dolomiti Meteo
- **Trail Conditions and Updates:** Local alpine clubs and tourist centers often provide updates on trail conditions.
  - **Alpenverein Südtirol (AVS):** AVS Website
  - **Club Alpino Italiano (CAI):** CAI Website

Travel Insurance

- Ensure you have comprehensive travel insurance that covers medical emergencies, evacuation, and adventure activities such as hiking, climbing, and skiing.

Local Guides and Tours

- **Certified Guides:** Hiring a local guide can enhance your experience and ensure safety on challenging trails. Look for guides certified by UIAGM/IFMGA.
  - **Dolomiti Guides:** Dolomiti Guides Website

Important Tips

- **Keep Important Numbers Handy:** Save emergency numbers and your insurance details in your phone and carry a written copy.
- **Stay Informed:** Regularly check weather forecasts and trail conditions.
- **First Aid Kit:** Always carry a basic first aid kit and know how to use it.
- **Emergency Plan:** Have a plan for what to do in case of an emergency, including knowing the location of the nearest shelter or rifugio.

Useful Phrases in Italian and German

When traveling in the Dolomites, you'll encounter both Italian and German-speaking locals, as well as Ladin speakers in some areas. Here are some useful phrases in Italian and German to help you navigate and communicate during your trip.

Basic Greetings

Italian:

- Hello: Ciao / Buongiorno (good morning)
- Good evening: Buonasera
- Goodbye: Arrivederci
- Please: Per favore
- Thank you: Grazie
- Yes: Sì
- No: No
- Excuse me: Mi scusi

German:

- Hello: Hallo / Guten Tag (good day)
- Good evening: Guten Abend
- Goodbye: Auf Wiedersehen
- Please: Bitte
- Thank you: Danke
- Yes: Ja
- No: Nein
- Excuse me: Entschuldigung

Directions

Italian:

- Where is…?: Dove si trova…?
- How do I get to…?: Come si arriva a…?
- Left: Sinistra
- Right: Destra
- Straight ahead: Dritto
- Near: Vicino
- Far: Lontano

German:

- Where is…?: Wo ist…?
- How do I get to…?: Wie komme ich zu…?
- Left: Links
- Right: Rechts
- Straight ahead: Geradeaus
- Near: In der Nähe
- Far: Weit

Accommodation

Italian:

- Do you have a room available?: Avete una camera disponibile?
- How much does it cost per night?: Quanto costa per notte?
- Can I see the room?: Posso vedere la camera?
- I have a reservation: Ho una prenotazione

German:

- Do you have a room available?: Haben Sie ein Zimmer frei?
- How much does it cost per night?: Wie viel kostet es pro Nacht?
- Can I see the room?: Kann ich das Zimmer sehen?
- I have a reservation: Ich habe eine Reservierung

Dining

Italian:

- A table for two, please: Un tavolo per due, per favore
- Can I see the menu?: Posso vedere il menu?
- What do you recommend?: Cosa mi consiglia?
- I am vegetarian: Sono vegetariano/a
- Check, please: Il conto, per favore

German:

- A table for two, please: Ein Tisch für zwei, bitte
- Can I see the menu?: Kann ich die Speisekarte sehen?
- What do you recommend?: Was empfehlen Sie?
- I am vegetarian: Ich bin Vegetarier/in
- Check, please: Die Rechnung, bitte

Shopping

Italian:

- How much is this?: Quanto costa questo?

- Do you accept credit cards?: Accettate carte di credito?
- I'm just looking: Sto solo guardando
- Can you help me?: Può aiutarmi?

German:

- How much is this?: Wie viel kostet das?
- Do you accept credit cards?: Akzeptieren Sie Kreditkarten?
- I'm just looking: Ich schaue nur
- Can you help me?: Können Sie mir helfen?

Emergencies

Italian:

- I need help: Ho bisogno di aiuto
- Call the police: Chiami la polizia
- Call an ambulance: Chiami un'ambulanza
- I'm lost: Mi sono perso/a

German:

- I need help: Ich brauche Hilfe
- Call the police: Rufen Sie die Polizei
- Call an ambulance: Rufen Sie einen Krankenwagen
- I'm lost: Ich habe mich verirrt

Transport

Italian:

- Where is the bus/train station?: Dove si trova la stazione degli autobus/treni?
- When does the next bus/train leave?: Quando parte il prossimo autobus/treno?
- One ticket to... please: Un biglietto per... per favore

German:

- Where is the bus/train station?: Wo ist der Busbahnhof/Bahnhof?
- When does the next bus/train leave?: Wann fährt der nächste Bus/Zug ab?
- One ticket to... please: Ein Ticket nach... bitte

Health and Wellness

Italian:

- I need a doctor: Ho bisogno di un dottore
- Is there a pharmacy nearby?: C'è una farmacia qui vicino?
- I feel sick: Mi sento male

German:

- I need a doctor: Ich brauche einen Arzt
- Is there a pharmacy nearby?: Gibt es eine Apotheke in der Nähe?
- I feel sick: Mir ist schlecht

Travel Insurance for the Dolomites

Travel insurance is essential when planning a trip to the Dolomites. It provides financial protection and peace of mind in case of unexpected events. Here's what you need to know about travel insurance and what it should cover.

Key Coverage Areas

1. Medical Coverage:

- **Emergency Medical Expenses:** Coverage for medical treatment in case of illness or injury.
- **Medical Evacuation:** Coverage for transportation to the nearest suitable medical facility.
- **Repatriation:** Coverage for transportation back to your home country if necessary.

2. Trip Cancellation and Interruption:

- **Trip Cancellation:** Reimbursement for prepaid expenses if you have to cancel your trip due to covered reasons (e.g., illness, injury, family emergency).
- **Trip Interruption:** Coverage for the unused portion of your trip if it is interrupted due to covered reasons.

3. Lost or Delayed Baggage:

- **Lost Baggage:** Reimbursement for personal belongings if your baggage is lost, stolen, or damaged.
- **Delayed Baggage:** Coverage for essential items if your baggage is delayed for a certain period.

4. Travel Delays:

- **Travel Delay:** Compensation for additional expenses if your trip is delayed for a covered reason.

5. Adventure Activities Coverage:

- **Hiking and Climbing:** Ensure your policy covers activities like hiking, climbing, and via ferrata routes.
- **Winter Sports:** Coverage for skiing, snowboarding, and other winter sports if traveling in winter.

6. Personal Liability:

- **Personal Liability:** Coverage for legal expenses and compensation if you accidentally cause injury to someone or damage their property.

Recommended Insurance Providers

Here are some well-known travel insurance providers that offer comprehensive coverage:

1. World Nomads:

- Known for covering adventure activities.
- Offers customizable plans.
- **Website:** World Nomads

2. Allianz Global Assistance:

- Offers a range of plans for different needs.
- Good coverage for medical expenses and trip interruptions.
- **Website:** Allianz Global Assistance

3. Travel Guard by AIG:

- Provides various plans with extensive coverage options.
- Good for comprehensive travel protection.
- **Website:** Travel Guard

4. InsureMyTrip:

- A comparison site to find the best travel insurance plan.
- Offers multiple providers and plan options.
- **Website:** InsureMyTrip

5. SafetyWing:

- Focuses on long-term travelers and digital nomads.
- Offers coverage for medical expenses and travel delays.
- **Website:** SafetyWing

Tips for Choosing Travel Insurance

1. Assess Your Needs:

- Consider the activities you plan to do and ensure they are covered.
- Think about your health, trip length, and the value of your belongings.

2. Compare Plans:

- Use comparison websites to evaluate different policies and providers.
- Look at coverage limits, exclusions, and deductibles.

3. Read the Fine Print:

- Understand what is covered and what is excluded.
- Check the claim process and required documentation.

4. Purchase Early:

- Buy insurance as soon as you book your trip to cover potential cancellations.
- Ensure you have coverage for the entire duration of your trip.

5. Keep Documentation:

- Keep copies of your insurance policy, emergency contact numbers, and receipts for any expenses you might claim.

By securing comprehensive travel insurance, you can protect yourself against unexpected events and enjoy your trip to the Dolomites with greater peace of mind.

Conclusion and Final Tips

The Dolomites offer a remarkable combination of natural beauty, outdoor adventure, and cultural richness. Whether you are hiking through stunning alpine meadows, exploring historic trails, or enjoying the local cuisine, this region provides an unforgettable experience. To ensure a safe and enjoyable trip, here are some final tips and key takeaways.

Final Tips

1. Plan Ahead:

- Research your routes, accommodation, and transportation options in advance.
- Make reservations for popular rifugios and hotels early, especially during peak seasons.

2. Pack Wisely:

- Prepare for variable weather conditions with layered clothing and waterproof gear.
- Carry essential hiking gear, including a first aid kit, map or GPS, and plenty of water and snacks.

3. Stay Safe:

- Stick to marked trails and be aware of your surroundings.
- Check weather forecasts regularly and be prepared for sudden changes.

- Inform someone of your plans and estimated return time.

4. Respect Nature:

- Follow Leave No Trace principles to protect the environment.
- Respect wildlife and local flora, and avoid disturbing natural habitats.

5. Embrace Local Culture:

- Learn a few basic phrases in Italian and German to communicate effectively with locals.
- Engage with local customs, try regional dishes, and visit cultural sites.

6. Secure Travel Insurance:

- Ensure you have comprehensive travel insurance that covers medical emergencies, trip cancellations, and adventure activities.
- Keep a copy of your insurance policy and emergency contact numbers with you.

7. Stay Informed:

- Visit tourist information centers for up-to-date advice and maps.
- Use reliable resources and apps for trail conditions and navigation.

8. Enjoy the Journey:

- Take your time to soak in the breathtaking views and the unique atmosphere of the Dolomites.
- Capture memories with photos, but also take moments to simply enjoy the natural beauty.

Conclusion

The Dolomites are a paradise for outdoor enthusiasts and nature lovers, offering endless opportunities for adventure and exploration. With careful planning, respect for the environment, and a sense of adventure, your trip to the Dolomites can be an extraordinary experience filled with awe-inspiring landscapes and lasting memories.

Embrace the beauty, challenge yourself on the trails, and immerse yourself in the rich culture of this stunning region. Whether you're trekking through the mountains, savoring local cuisine, or discovering historical sites, the Dolomites promise an unforgettable journey. Happy travels!

MAPES.

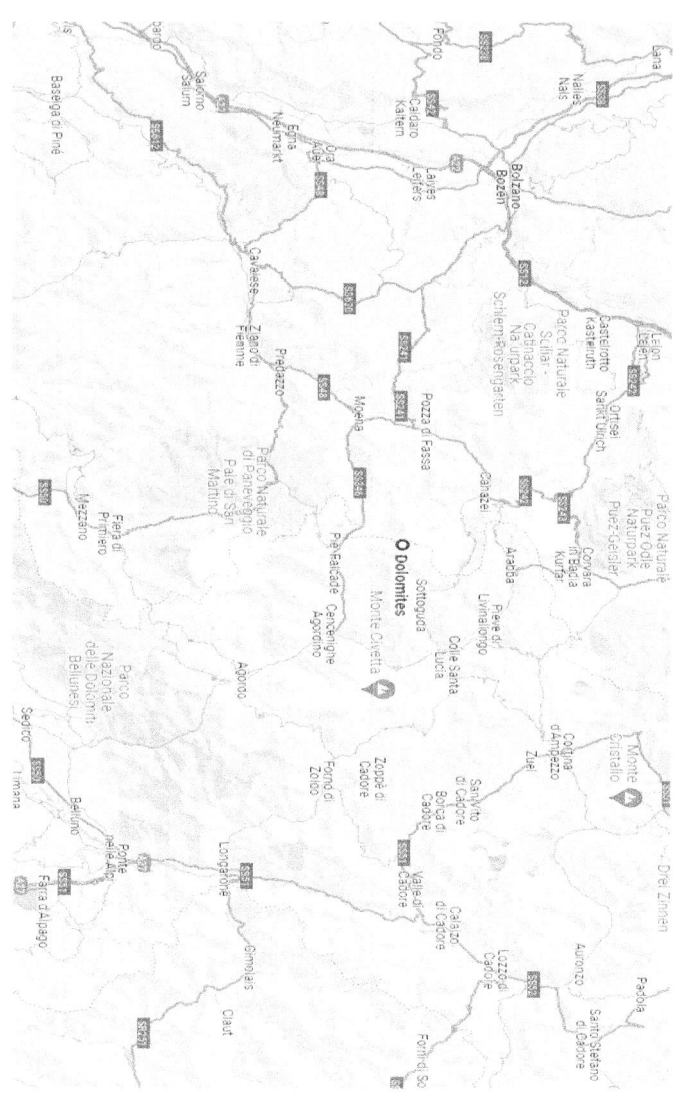

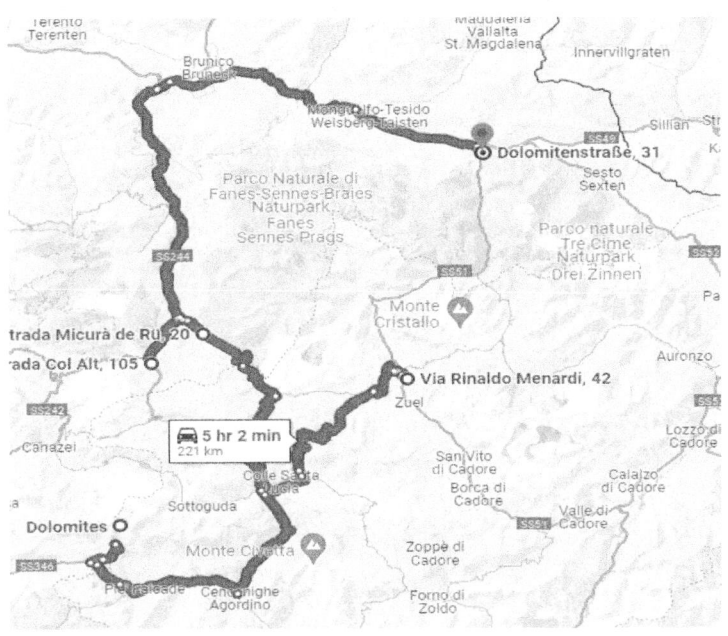

 click here to view map

Printed in Great Britain
by Amazon